THE SOUL WITHIN

DIANE WRIGHT

BALBOA.PRESS

A DIVISION OF HAY HOUSE

Balboa Press books may be ordered through booksellers or by contacting:

Balboa Press
A Division of Hay House
1663 Liberty Drive
Bloomington, IN 47403
www.balboapress.co.uk
UK TFN: 0800 0148647 (Toll Free inside the UK)
UK Local: (02) 0369 56325 (+44 20 3695 6325 from outside the UK)

Print information available on the last page.

ISBN: 978-1-9822-8862-4 (sc)
ISBN: 978-1-9822-8863-1 (hc)
ISBN: 978-1-9822-8861-7 (e)

Library of Congress Control Number: 2024908005

Balboa Press rev. date: 04/22/2024

CONTENTS

ACKNOWLEDGEMENTS

I'm jumping for joy and bursting with gratitude as I write this book-venture. None of this would've been possible without the amazing humans that surround me! A huge round of applause to my fabulous clients, who over the years have shown boundless enthusiasm and energy for reflexology. You guys are the reason I'm able to share stories that make us laugh, cry, and, most importantly, smooth out the ripples of life. Big thanks to my spellbinding teachers who fed my thirst for knowledge, sending me down rabbit holes of questions, and to the special souls that crossed my path, becoming amazing friends and opening doors of opportunity along the way. Patricia Christie and Melanie Cruickshank, a shout-out to you for letting me show off my treatments at my first trade show. Louise Blakeley, you rock! Not only did you welcome me into your home, but you also gave me the chance to work and travel—my ultimate passion. Tracey Buckley at Kelso, you believed in me and my treatments, and we shared so much from horses to spas. Big shout out to Isa Machado, my Earth warrior who transformed my journey in New Zealand with epic road trips and endless giggles! Clare Markey, your passion and determination are unmatched (even if you do insist on telling me what I need to buy!). Chris Jackson, those endless laughs in the camper vans, through wind or rain, were everything. A massive shout-out goes to the NHS staff, true angels who show dedication, love, and support every day, and to all the surgeons. Without your work, I wouldn't be here sharing my story. A true friend of mine, Angela Giovannini, has been my rock during my work and writing of this book, promising no more drafts to check at silly o'clock! To my fantastic folks, Nancy and Michael, it was quite a ride! I'm not sure this is what you had in mind when you wished for a daughter but thank you for being my rock and supporting me every step of the way. I love you to infinity and beyond! And to my blue-eyed brother, Steven, I'm always here for you. And to his wife, Tara; my super niece, Tiea; and my nephew, George, keep doing what you love. Let's keep spreading love and gratitude, peeps! Oh, finally, you—the seeker of joy! A wanderer on the path of inspiration! Your gaze has found its way to this book of light and wonder, and I speak to you, dear adventurer. Within these pages I hope you find keys to unlock the gates of purest joy and happiness, and for all who seek inspiration. I, too, have journeyed on this quest, and it is a privilege to share with you on my path.

Love and Light,

Diane x

FOREWORD

In a world where each of us walks our own unique and bumpy path, there are moments when we encounter stories that resonate deeply within our hearts, inspiring us to embrace life with renewed vigor and optimism. Diane Wright's autobiography is one such narrative, a remarkable journey that traverses the highs and lows of existence with unwavering resilience and boundless compassion.

Over the years I have known Diane, I have found myself captivated by the authenticity of her voice and the depth of her experiences. From her humble beginnings in the picturesque landscapes of Northumberland, UK, to the bustling highways of Europe, Diane's journey unfolds like a favourite patchwork quilt with threads of adventure, and where each square is another story of perseverance and profound self-discovery.

Born with an indomitable spirit and an insatiable thirst for life, Diane's early years were marked by a sense of wanderlust and curiosity, traits which I think are exactly the reason we connected so well. From a young age, she possessed an innate ability to embrace change and adapt to new circumstances with grace and resilience, qualities that would serve her well in the years to come.

But it was during her battle with health issues that Diane's true strength and resilience were put to the test. Confronted with the daunting reality of a Lupus diagnosis, she refused to be defined by her illness, instead choosing to embark on a journey of holistic healing and self-discovery. It was through this journey that Diane discovered her true calling as a healer, using her own experiences to guide and inspire others on their path to wellness.

Throughout her autobiography, Diane shares candidly the challenges she faced, from navigating the uncertainties of chronic illness to finding purpose and meaning in the face of adversity. Yet, through it all, her unwavering optimism and unyielding determination shine brightly, serving as a beacon of hope for all who encounter her story.

But Diane's narrative isn't just about overcoming obstacles; it's about embracing life with open arms and finding joy in the journey, no matter how winding the road may be.

Through her words, she reminds us that life is a precious gift, meant to be cherished and savored with every breath and that even in the darkest of moments, there exists the potential for growth, transformation, and renewal.

As you journey through the pages of Diane's remarkable story, I invite you to open your heart to the beauty of life's journey, to find solace in the face of adversity, and to embrace the magic that surrounds us each day.

For in Diane's tale, we find not only the courage to overcome our own obstacles but also the wisdom to appreciate the beauty of the present moment and the strength to forge ahead with unwavering hope and determination.

So in the pages that lie ahead, allow yourself to absorb the extraordinary life of Diane Wright, a true embodiment of strength, resilience, and unwavering optimism. May her story inspire you to embrace life's challenges with courage and grace, and to find joy in every twist and turn along the way.

With heartfelt admiration,
Nikki Collinson-Phenix

INTRODUCTION

Meet Diane, a luminary with a heart of gold who's just like you! She's a spunky gal who knows how to take on life's curveballs, even when it means shifting gears. With her magical reflexology skills and years of holistic therapy, she's a healing guru who crafts bespoke prescriptions for her clients. Her autobiography is not just about the good stuff. It's about squeezing the juice out of life, taking risks, and chasing your dreams. When the going gets tough, and you feel stuck in a rut, take a breath, look around, and feel the love around you. Trust us; someone else is fighting a tougher battle. Life's too short for rehearsals, and we don't come with an expiry date. Her humble beginnings in Northumberland, UK, Diane has done it all, including helping people with disabilities, booking flights and holidays, and serving as a community police officer, Diane also hit the road, driving lorries across Europe but when health issues threw a wrench into her plans, a diagnosis of lupus, an autoimmune disease, led her to reflexology, and she hasn't looked back since. After a kidney transplant, Diane's healing skills took her across the globe. Her story is a powerful one of self-discovery, resilience, and the sheer strength of female power. It will inspire you to grab life by the horns and make every moment count.

Diane x

CHAPTER 1

From an incredibly early age, I became familiar with hospitals. At just eleven months old, I was taken to one to undergo tests to determine the cause of my prolonged illness. My parents were understandably concerned and anxious, especially as it was their first time experiencing such a situation with their newborn. I have no recollection of the worry that they must have felt and I know I will never fully understand what it is like for parents to see their children in pain and distress. However, I know that the healing power of being part of a loving family is crucial in such situations. After various tests, doctors suspected that I might have coeliac disease, which would have meant an intolerance to gluten and wheat. However, further tests proved this theory incorrect, and I was allowed to go home. In the following weeks, I regained the weight I had lost and began to thrive like any other toddler. Despite there being no clear explanation for my earlier illness, I was quite a healthy child.

Memories of this time were to profoundly affect me for years to come. My memories related in this book commenced around age two.

My parents lived in a small hamlet near Hexham, Northumberland. The colonel and his family owned the houses and surrounding ground. The colonel had lived within the area for years and they occupied the main house on the estate with their family. Large oak trees bordered the area, and the ground was overwhelmed by seasonal flowers either around the gardens or popping out of the walls between the two houses where my parents lived. Our garden was quite small, with grass and a few flower beds dotted around the garden path. The washing line was always full of fresh, clean clothes blowing in the breeze. At the back door was a small yard, across which was the toilet and another outhouse, where garden tools were kept. The kitchen had small workbenches and cupboards inside the back door and additional storage under the sink was where the bath was! The kitchen was a sanctuary for smells of home cooking, including ginger biscuits and fresh scones.

Next door to our house were my Aunty Helen and Uncle Billy—not my real aunt and uncle, but their status remained for years to follow. Uncle Billy loved his garden, where fresh fruit and vegetables would be on hand. Billy also took magnificent pleasure in his vegetable patch. His leeks were his pride and joy and continual hard work enabled him to win local events and shows. Wednesday would be the feasting night, when Aunty Helen and Uncle Billy would prepare their unique specialty—leek pudding! This was a savoury dish comprising fresh leeks and vegetables and crowned with a pastry topping. The evenings would be spent chatting over the past few days' activities. Uncle Billy and my father would discuss anything from the garden to new television equipment that would become available for the home, whereas Aunty Helen and my mother would chat about family life. My father had served his apprenticeship as a television engineer and was now working full-time for a local company. Television was going through a revolution at that time, changing from black-and-white to high-tech colour television sets. My father later went on to set up his television and aerial repair business. As Uncle Billy addressed his garden, Aunty Helen would formulate the best ginger biscuits, a title that remains to date. The only advice I remember from Aunty Helen a few years later was always to have some ginger biscuits in the house, as they are an excellent ingredient for an upset tummy. This recipe is still used to date along with Aunty Helen's Women's Institute recipes.

My parents rented a house from the colonel, who lived with his family in what I knew as the big house. My mother agreed to maintain the colonel's farm accounts every week to rent our house. The entire estate was like a page from a fairy tale book with every turn revealing new and exciting paths and walkways. The driveway seemed endless, curving right and left and as a child, my little legs would always tire before I reached the grand house.

Now, I know you are reading this thinking, "How can she remember these memories?" I can already see you scratching your head, wondering how I remember this stuff! Believe me; I know it sounds unbelievable. But trust me; it is legit!

As I began drafting this book, it felt as if I were being transported back to a dream-like state, reliving those precious memories. It was like watching a magical film unfold in slo-mo, and I did not want to leave that wonderful moment. So I dare you to dig deep and recollect your own cherished childhood memories!

My mother weaves stories of my childhood; she recalls a time when, even as a youngling, I fiercely rejected the notion of handholding, a proclamation of self-sufficiency. My grandparents, too, noted this fire within me and whispered tales of how I seemed to have lived this life before, possessing a wisdom beyond my age.

Those were the glory days! Strolling up the driveway was like setting out on a daring escapade. My tiny legs would give out eventually, and I'd have to beg my mum to carry me or ride in a pushchair. But let's be honest; sometimes I'd just lose my cool and throw a tantrum.

Spring was the best time, with snowdrops and daffodils carpeting the ground, and bluebells following close behind. The air was thick with the sweet scent of freshly cut grass, animals, flowers, and garlic. I could not resist running my hands over the garlic leaves, but then I would have to be rubbed down with dock leaves to get the smell off! At the end of the drive was the stable block, with its reddish sandstone and wooden doors, some with metal railings so the horses could peek out. The horses inside were always friendly, but my fearless approach sent my mother's blood pressure soaring! The smell of sweet horses mixed with good old manure filled the air, and I could not resist sneaking over to say hi. The towering trees that ran alongside the drive to the house were so tall it felt as though they could touch the sky.

The house flaunted colossal windows, and doors that took ages to budge and echoed like a castle. I can still recall the black-and-white chequered floor that greeted me at the entrance, leading to a warm, cosy kitchen. The Aga oven roared like a beast, pumping out heat, while three or four black Labradors wrestled for a spot near the fire.

The house had forbidden rooms, ones I was never to set foot in, including the colonel's private pad and the office. But oh, boy, did those grown-up spaces have an eye-boggling floral print! I swear, if you looked too hard, you would see birds flapping around the cushion covers!

In my recollection, the colonel was an imposing figure whose towering presence and benevolent countenance commanded attention. He had a shock of white hair that was swept back from his eyes, and his robust physique betokened great strength. Even when he stood next to a window, his stature filled the room, and the windows stretched skyward.

As my mum crunched numbers, I got to sneak off to the children's playroom. Oh, the treasures hidden inside! There were dollhouses, toys, and my personal favourite, the mighty rocking horse. With a little help from my mum, I would clamber atop Dapple, the magnificent dapple-grey stallion with its flowing white mane. And guess what? I still cannot resist a grey horse to this day.

I was gutted that I never got to hop onto the tan saddle; my legs could not even reach the stirrups! But if I had made it, I would have felt like a wild adventurer galloping through the nursery. My new bud was Dapple, and my faithful sidekick was Bobby, the family Labrador. Imagine a giant, fluffy, gold teddy bear towering over you. That was Bobby, who could easily pass as a majestic horse. But he was just a big, old softie who loved a good belly rub. Together we ran wild through my toddler days! From the get-go, I realized my new BFF was a dog, not a horse, so no piggyback rides for me. Instead, we played a game of tag, for which I was down. I loved all animals, whether they had hooves or fur, but the horses stole my heart.

One bright spring morning when I was barely three years old, someone came knocking at our door. My mum went to peek through the letterbox and a majestic 16.2hh hunter-type horse stood right in front of her. Guess who was accompanying this regal creature? None other than the colonel himself! His words of wisdom? "Start them young!"

Ringo was a stunning creature with a rich dun coat and deep brown eyes that could hypnotize anybody. The most striking feature was the bold white stripe that ran across his face, paired with two crisp white socks. His coat varied from his face to his neck, with the latter being smoother and lighter in shade, whereas his neck and underbelly were sharper to the touch—a reminder of his recent clip. He looked like a glamorous model walking down the runway!

My new friend Ringo had come fresh from the fields, sporting his trusty New Zealand rug to keep him warm and dry. He was a remarkable sight, with a mud-caked head collar and all! My mum was gobsmacked, lost for words. But the colonel had a plan. "Quick, grab a tea towel; that'll do for now." It was a hilarious scene! Her heart was pounding like a drum solo as a million thoughts raced in her head. She whirled around and made a beeline for the nearest tea towel. How was she going to keep her cool? He was like a skyscraper towering over her! Picture this: outside the garden gate, the colonel gave my mother a quick tutorial on how to manage Ringo, asking her to hold his lead rope while he helped me onto Ringo's back. With one hand clutching a towel and the other my coat, we waltzed down the garden path. It was a bumpy start, but I clung on for dear life, grabbing a handful of mane as if I were hanging onto a wild bull! Luckily, my mother was there to steady me as Ringo trotted off down the lane. It was like a scene out of some daring nursery rhyme! My dear mother still marvels at how he managed to keep my balance, but we pulled it off like pros!

I was living the dream, with not a single worry in sight, when suddenly the colonel and Ringo whisked in for a regular visit. I was a natural jockey, yearning to take the reins and hold on tight for the ride of my life. I recall thinking, "Wow, that's a long way to the ground!" But with Ringo by my side, even at the tender age of three, I felt safe and secure. His watchful eye kept me from harm's way, and to this day, those memories are as vivid as if they happened yesterday.

In the cosy riding cottage, we made ourselves at home for about three and a half years. But soon my parents decided to pack up and move to the next village over, Acomb. Lucky for me, I made a new friend and gained a bro in the process. Steven showed up right as we moved into our brand-new house on a fresh, uncharted estate. I still remember the muddy path that led to our doorstep, as the proper road had not been laid yet. We were pioneers of the new turf! The estate was a mix of old and new houses, and some that were still under construction. It was my first time attending Acomb School, and while I enjoyed it at first, being told what to do was not really my jam. I am always up for trying new things, but when I would ask the whys behind certain ways of doing things, I would get zilch. It was as if the answer were hiding in a black hole! Why wouldn't these adults just tell me? But I did make some amazing friends, especially Katherine, who became my BFF. We spent hours together, raiding her sister's dressing-up box. One day, we went all out and tried on everything new we could find, leaving clothes, shoes, skirts, and jumpers scattered all over the floor. To our surprise, we did not break our ankles trying on those high-heeled platforms! It was a mystery, but we sure had a blast!

CHAPTER 2

I was all set to start a new chapter in my life, both at home and school. But soon after we moved to Acomb, something strange began happening with one of my eyes. Yep, it was being a bit lazy or squinty, and off to the optician I went. After a few visits, the verdict was in—I had a lazy eye. All I remember from that time was a visit to the "grumpy lady" at the hospital. She struck fear into my trembling heart. As I stepped into the antiseptic-scented room, my nostrils flared in protest—a sensation I had come to call "the nose smell." Suddenly the cantankerous woman, who was usually perched behind a massive reception desk, materialized before me. Her long white coat billowed like a ghostly apparition, and her hand beckoned me to the "big chair room." I followed, my nerves quivering like leaves in a storm. Nestled in the corner, a small pristine sink sparkled, adorned with delightful trinkets that danced along the shelf. Above it, a mirror gazed back, reflecting the enchanting scene. A grand wooden desk stood at the heart of the room, accompanied by an immense chair that dominated the space. A wooden case cradling an assortment of delicate, silver-framed glass pieces glistened above, flanked by sheets of parchment. Gleaming silver instruments stood sentinel on a towering metal trolley. Despite the whimsical surroundings, the woman who occupied the room never seemed to grace it with a smile—a curious mystery that tugged at the heartstrings.

A massive oblong tube with a rope attached to the desk caught my eye. With a tug, the tube spun around, revealing various letters and pictures on each side. Although the top images were clear, the ones at the bottom seemed to vanish or were hiding on the other side. And oh, my goodness, the black chair was colossal! I needed a lift just to hop on! To ensure direct eye contact, a special seat was constructed, which involved adding a large piece of wood across both armrests. Throughout the meeting, I experienced a sense of anxiety and felt overwhelmed. As the lady asked me questions, I was instructed to remain still and listen attentively. However, I struggled to respond adequately, either nodding or shaking my head, unsure of what the right answer was.

I still shudder thinking about the moment she plonked those massive glasses on my wee face. The metal frames were so big they could have doubled as a bicycle wheel, and the round lenses were like mini magnifying glasses! It was like being trapped in a horror film for a minute. As they rested on my nose, I felt as if I were carrying a ton of bricks, and my nose was being pushed to my forehead! Then she would cover one eye with a black card and ask, "Is it clearer like this or like that?" She showed me all sorts of things, including animals and shades of red and green. By the end of it all, I was still seeing spots dancing before my eyes even as I walked out of the appointment. I was a frequent visitor to the hospital before being admitted to Walkergate Hospital in Newcastle upon Tyne. The doctors confirmed that I had to undergo a small eye operation to fix my squint. At the age of four, I had no idea what was coming next. I donned a pirate patch over my eye following the operation, which I did not like, as none of the other kids at school had one. But my parents kept telling me how special I was and that nobody had a pirate patch like me. Despite their words, I always tried to remove it and got upset at the thought of looking like a pirate.

Back in the seventies, the National Health Service had limited options for glasses, with only three colours available: blue, pink, and brown. Luck had it that the brown colour suited me the most, as I had deep brown curly hair, however, a downside was that my hair had a mind of its own and was always tightly curled, adding to the list of troubles I faced in my early days. Deep brown glasses, a pirate patch and curly hair—glamorous it was not!

Back in the good old days of Acomb, we celebrated Queen Elizabeth II's Silver Jubilee with the most epic street parties! It was like a never-ending summer, with sunshine all around. I cannot recall even a single rainy day. I was hibernating during those dull days! The festivities went on forever, with nonstop bash after bash and extraordinary events galore. Those were the days! One of my most vivid memories of street parties was the celebration of the Silver Jubilee, during which all the primary school children were seated together to enjoy an array of delicious food prepared by their parents. The table, extending the length of the school playing field, was adorned with various dishes, including large mixing bowls filled to the brim with wobbly jelly. The Tupperware boxes brimmed with crisps and sausage rolls overflowed. Unlimited sandwiches were served, with some crusts removed to cater for fussy children. Of course, no party is complete without ice cream, and that's where Mr. Whippy's ice cream van came in. We were directed to leave our tables and collect our ice cream. The whole venue was adorned with red, white, and blue colours, with flags and bunting draped across every chair and table, completing the festive ambiance. The older children were tasked with performing a maypole dance while adorned in their finest party attire, each clutching his or her respective ribbon. As the music commenced, the children gracefully executed their choreographed routine to the delight of the audience. I could not help but appreciate the older children's impressive memory and coordination skills. However, I realized that if I were ever asked to perform a similar feat, I would have to plead for an exemption, as I was not blessed with such aptitude.

CHAPTER 3

My horse-related activities ceased when we relocated from the riding cottage to Acomb. However, my insistence on resuming them persisted. On my fourth Christmas, my parents gifted me with my first pair of riding boots and riding lessons. The lessons were conducted at a small riding school in Hexham Shire, managed by a remarkable lady named Jane. Meet Jane Dotchin—a tiny ball of fiery energy. She was a lover of the great outdoors and lived off the grid with her trusty terrier squad and four ponies. Life was simple, yet perfect. Imagine fresh veggies growing right in her backyard and ponies wandering around the charming stone abode—pure bliss! The horse stalls were the spot for brushing and getting everything in order. Jane's techniques were so effortlessly grasped that even a young girl like me could become a horse-whisperer in no time! At first, Jane's pony lessons were as chill as a sloth in a hammock. We started with the basics, learning how to groom and care for these majestic creatures, and then, finally, it was time to saddle up, giddy up, and trot like a pro. We took to the main roads to get a feel for the traffic, and boy, did we turn heads! I bet if my parents knew about these epic adventures, they would have begged to come along. Sometimes we did not even know where we would be galloping off to until the day, adding to the thrill of the ride. On the rare occasion that we did know, it was because we were going on a full-blown, four-hour expedition through the breathtaking countryside of Hexham Shire. Yee-haw! Back in the day, we would gear up for adventure by packing a rucksack with goodies, such as our favourite lunch, juice boxes, and an extra raincoat (just in case Mother Nature had other plans).If we needed to refuel while gallivanting, we would swing by Jane's friend's farm, where they would light up a crackling fire and cook up the tastiest sausages over the flames. As the tea kettle boiled, we would all pitch in with tasks like pony wrangling and firewood collecting, making the day that much more memorable. The ponies, meanwhile, were left to bask in the sun and munch on grass to their hearts' content. Under her tutelage, I received exceptional guidance in horsemanship while imbibing a tenacious spirit, encouraging me to pursue my dreams at an early age. Despite facing numerous setbacks, Jane went on to travel the length and breadth of the UK on horseback. Her unwavering positivity and determination to overcome daily challenges left a profound impact on me from an early age, which continues to inspire me to this day. Ah, reminiscing about the golden days! Although some of our youthful exploits may raise eyebrows today, those moments of unfettered spontaneity opened doors that forever altered the courses of our lives. My friend Jane was a veritable treasure trove of tales from her younger years, including her recounting of how she tamed wild ponies by falling off them repeatedly. Her mantra was simple: "Rise again, brush off the dust, and keep forging ahead!" For if we shy away from risks, we will be left behind, wondering about the paths not taken. We were always game for any adventure on our horse-riding escapades. It was all about taking life by the horns, tumbling, getting up, and learning it all over again, while having some good old giggles in the middle. It is funny how that motto has stuck with me all these years. I was under Jayne's tutelage for three years, and boy was it a blast! I am a bit hazy about why we stopped, but we had to pack up and move on to a new chapter in my parents' lives.

CHAPTER 4

Let us time-travel to 1979, where we were all set to kickstart a new chapter in a wee village called Newbrough, Northumberland. Our humble abode was to be a jolly old pub named the Red Lion, which had been my grandparents' nest for a solid two decades until they retired. Growing up, I was blessed to have both sets of grandparents around, and boy, did they make my teenage years rock! Let us turn back time and meet the epic grandparents who made our world a better place. On one side, we have the dynamic duo George and Ethel Wright, who rocked the Red Lion pub scene by creating a haven for working-class folks to hang out and have fun. On the other side, we have Des and Jean Craigie, the unstoppable pair who proved that hard work and love go hand in hand, making every single day an occasion to celebrate.

I considered being remarkably close to Grandmother Jean during my childhood years. She was always a classically dressed lady whose makeup was always perfect and who attended a weekly keep fit class to maintain her figure. Grandfather Des was small in stature and had a great love for his garden and carpet bowls. His approach to life involved sayings about saving money for a rainy day. My granny Ethel was the life and soul of the party, always up for a good joke and a laugh. People used to say I looked exactly like her when she was young, and I never got it until I saw old photos of her. With her dark complexion and almost black hair, she always looked as if she had just gotten back from a trip abroad. And boy, did she love to travel! Even though my grandpa George would not fly with her, she would jet off with her gal friends and explore the world. She had the craziest tales of flying on planes that looked as though they were about to take a nosedive! But her ultimate dream was to visit the USA, and she finally made it happen. Those stories were her absolute favourite and stayed with her for life, ever since her childhood days.

My grandpa George was a sturdy fella with mitts the size of shovels! He had a wild passion for nature, hunting, and everything countryside related. He was my hero, and his life philosophy was pure gold: believe in yourself, chase your dreams, and never, ever give up. The word "impossible" was not even in his vocabulary! The lessons I learned at my grandparents' knees gave me the grit and determination I needed to conquer life's challenges. I often think about these and what George would say and do in the presence of life's curveballs. They were the ultimate travel guides on my journey. Way back in the day, when I was still a little sprout of eight or nine, my Grandpa George was quite the car enthusiast. He owned these massive, robust cars that made me feel as if I were embarking on a grand adventure just to climb into them! We were on our way to see Grandma when Grandpa suddenly pulled over on a narrow country lane. He then turned to me and asked whether I wanted to take the wheel! What a wild ride! Without hesitation, I scrambled over to the driver's seat and got ready for Grandpa's instructions. I could not get my legs to reach the pedals, so a fishing bag was procured from the boot. This was placed on the seat, which gave me an extra lift, allowing me to use my feet to work the three pedals. Grandpa shifted it into first gear, and I gently eased off the clutch, causing us to bop up and down like playful bunnies. My heart was thumping like a bass drum, leaving me speechless while Grandpa chatted away and I just gave him awkward nods and grunts. I had not been driving long when there in front of us was a small motorhome making its way along this narrow road. oh, my days! *Grandpa, what will I do?* Sheer panic flooded my body. Keeping his cool, he instructed me to keep close to the edge and keep going. The motorhome passed us gingerly, but all was good. Closer to Grandma's, we pulled over for Grandpa to take the reins again. Once we landed back at Grandma's house, we spilled the morning's wild events to her and boy did she give him a piece of her mind!

But hey, let us give credit where credit is due. These teeny-tiny yet mighty moments were the true heavyweights moulding me then—and even now! Dreams are the heart and soul of personal growth, and the bigger, the better! So go ahead and let your imagination run wild and aim for the stars when it comes to your life goals.

Once upon a time, the historic Red Lion Inn stood in a small village nestled amidst sprawling country houses and farms. With a history dating back to the 1400s, it was rumoured that even Bonnie Prince Charlie had once graced its halls. Its location on the Stanegate, a Roman marvel, only added to its charm. Generations of folks had flocked to this popular gathering spot, where socializing and fun were always on the menu. As soon as you step into the main bar area, you are greeted by a wild bunch of stuffed animals and antique horse brasses, each with its own tale to tell. The black beams above run across the whole bar, and a modern beam effect sneaks its way into the lounge, making for a perfect fusion of old and new. It is the kind of place that has kept its charm for decades, with intricate woodwork and shelves lined with bottles of the finest aged whisky. Step into the pub, and you will be transported into a magical world of mirrors! They are arranged so skilfully that you will feel as though you are peering into a never-ending drinking wonderland. The crown jewel of the place is the original sandstone fireplace, which is always alight, ready to warm up any cold soul. For years, the table beside the hearth has been a hub of good times, with locals gathering to share a beer and a game of dominos. The lounge is just off the main bar and is named after one of the Queen Mother's legendary racehorses. The tables are sturdy, with intricate metal designs and wooden tops. It is the perfect place to unwind and soak up the cosy ambiance. The Red Lion had that old-world charm, with little hints of its age sprinkled both inside and out.

When you step into the bar, it is as if you have travelled back in time, with the stables and hay barn right at the back. Once upon a time, horses and carriages would clippety-clop through the arch and onto the cobbles, settling in for a cosy night. I still remember how pristine the white-washed arch and the cobbled yard looked when we first arrived. My mind kept galloping towards a single dream—owning a pony! And guess what? Our family had stables!

CHAPTER 5

After years of convincing my parents, it was my Grandpa George who finally caved in. I was only six when I became the proud parent of a cream-coloured 12.2hh pony named HOBO. He had already been a star at the Pony Club, so I knew he was going to be my best friend for the next six years. We let him be his playful self, and he was never disappointed! My mum and I took leisurely strolls down the serene country roads with my trusty pony, Hobo, in tow. I thought I could go solo, but my mum would not hear of it! To prove her point, she hopped on a horse named Copper—a chill chestnut mare standing at 14.2hh. She was so calm and collected that you could have mistaken her for a stuffed animal!

Years flew by, and I became a Hobo expert, wandering the countryside like a boss. But my life took a wild turn when I joined the Pony Club, where I created some of my most memorable childhood moments. Novices and pro riders—we were all in it together, cheering each other on. The events were held at various local farms, where we started our days with some intense training sessions, followed by thrilling jumping competitions or gymkhana games. While I was not particularly fond of the training bit, we had our own little area, and it was a blast to follow each other around and trot off. Picture this: a group of little riders trotting around, cantering, and walking, with the instructor yelling, "Heels down! Stop kicking! Sit straight!" Cue the drama: ponies not behaving, kids having off days, and moms running around playing therapist. Amidst the chaos, I discovered something new: a funny accent! Our pony club was a melting pot of different folks, and boy, did we have a blast.

As a young rider, I had noticed something odd: the farmer's kids spoke the same language as I, but some of my fellow horse enthusiasts sounded as if they were talking through their noses! Bizarre, right? When I asked my mum about it, she said it could be an annoying cold. That stuck with me, but so did the farm's spirit of optimism, even during the occasional tumbles and scrapes. I, for one, was no stranger to minor mishaps, from being thrown off a pony to getting a hoof to the gut. But nothing could keep us from galloping back into the saddle! On a sun-kissed day at the pony club, my heart soared with joy as the morning unfolded flawlessly—no falls, no tears, and no tantrums. Adorning my feet were the newest addition to my riding ensemble— ankle boots with delicate elastic bands hugging my ankles.

After a delightful lunch with my equine companion, I sat beside a dear friend, relishing the afternoon's upcoming delights. Suddenly, with no warning, my friend's pony unleashed a vicious kick towards my beloved Hobo. The impact was swift and merciless, striking my ankle and causing a searing pain that surged towards my knee. My eyes brimmed with tears as concerned mothers rushed towards me, their hearts heavy with worry and uncertainty. An excursion to the hospital was deemed necessary to ascertain the extent of the damage. Upon my arrival, a nurse ushered me into a diminutive chamber whilst my mother relayed the details of my ordeal. Together with the nurses, she aided in removing my cherished new boot, which had become a source of both physical and emotional distress. I gazed in wonderment as they carefully severed the elastic bindings that held it in place. The ensuing X-ray confirmed a slight fracture in the ankle joint, and with the application of the plaster, the pain became an alien sensation, as if my ankle no longer belonged to me.

My childhood had some amazing moments, including my hunting escapades and my time at the Pony Club events. But the most unforgettable part occurred just before my eleventh birthday, when the pony club was on the hunt for new riders to train for the gymkhana games team. It was a mixed-age and mixed-ability group of about fifteen of us, all eager to make the cut. Watching the ponies gallop around, it seemed as if they knew the game better than we riders! We would all gather on a Sunday afternoon to catch up on the latest gossip and train. Six poles would be placed in a straight line, and we would be put through our paces to see who was the fastest to hop on a moving pony or who had the most confidence in the games. Those were the days!

The years that followed the games were the last with my trusty steed, Hobo. I had outgrown him and graduated to bigger horses. We had a few horses after Hobo, each with its own unique size, colour, and temperament. My mother and I eventually shared a horse named Sophie, a stunning strawberry roan mare who stood tall at 15hh. Now, Sophie had her little backstory. She had spent time in the traveller's environment and would sometimes get spooked by her shadow. Nonetheless, she was a lovely horse and loved to gallop across the countryside. Unfortunately, one fateful morning, I went to bring her in from the field and found her surrounded by the other horses, who had their heads bowed down. It was a tough moment, as I knew she had passed away. I quickly told my mother, and the slaughterhouse was called. This moment will stay with me forever, as it was on my sixteenth birthday. After this, I thought I was done with the horse world, but life had other plans.

CHAPTER 6

My high school graduation was a bittersweet moment filled with both cheerful and melancholic vibes. I knew I would miss my friends who were either heading to university or staying back at school. But one thing was clear: I had no desire to continue studying in either college or university. I was eager to dive into the working world and earn some dough.

That's when I heard of the groovy new YTS programme, a youth training scheme that was all the rage in 1988–1989. And guess what? I seized the day and signed up for an outdoor activity instructor course at a centre for those with disabilities and mental health challenges. It was an opportunity to have influence and learn some wicked skills! Nestled beside the breathtaking Kielder Water in Northumberland, you will find the Calvert Trust—a hidden gem! The whole area is a nature lover's paradise, with dense forests and Europe's largest freshwater dam. You will never run out of things to do, with endless trails to hike and cycle. The Calvert Trust is the perfect sanctuary for both patients and caregivers, whether they want to unwind in the countryside or dive into one of the many activities on offer. The trust has everything you need for a comfortable stay, including an indoor swimming pool and a top-notch dialysis unit. Speaking of which, the dialysis unit was, without trouble, my favourite feature during my stay. While patients patiently dialyzed, I would often share tales of the local dam or interesting titbits about the area. In exchange, they would open up about their past and present lives, painting a vivid picture of their world beyond the clinic. The sheer grit and drive of these patients left an impression on me during my early years. Back then, we would take them on a quick trip outside Kielder village to an old kiln. It was a sandstone beauty with two arches flanking a central wall where they once burnt lime. This was the spot where we would take our abseiling game to the next level! I will never forget the first time I saw it. The special wheelchair designed for our disabled customers looked like a regular one, but with a little extra metal to help with the ropes and gear. Safety was our top priority, and we always made sure everything ran smoothly. Our expert instructors even walked alongside each customer on the opposite side of the chair. It was a thrilling ride without a single oops! We witnessed pure joy as we guided them down the wall and into the arms of our cheerful team at the bottom. Looks of pure bliss spread across their faces, and they could not help but burst with excitement. Every single person who took this journey had a story to tell, and it was always the hot topic of the night! The fun and excitement would lift any mood in the centre. The Calvert Trust is where I truly found both my feet and adulthood. I learned so much from both fellow instructors and customers equally during my time spent in Kielder at the Calvert Trust. I also remember thinking during my early days at the Calvert Trust how lucky I was to have all my body parts in good working order, getting about my daily work without help. How these words would haunt me in only a few years' time. Unfortunately, the YTS position was to end after two years, but it was the most inspiring and uplifting two years of my life, and for that reason, I would like to say a huge thank-you to all concerned.

I came crashing back to reality as I returned to my parents' home at the Red Lion. Suddenly I was all grown up and had to figure out my next steps. I was completely lost and had no clue what to do next. I missed my training at Kielder and wished I could continue there forever. But instead, I found myself helping at the Red Lion, which was nice but not exactly my calling. I yearned for adventure and excitement, but what it looked like I had no idea. Even to this day, that dream remains a mystery.

CHAPTER 7

Amidst the bustling charm of the Town Moore in Newcastle upon Tyne. The Town Moor is an area of common land in Newcastle upon Tyne. It covers an area of 1000 acres, making it larger than Hyde Park and Hampstead heath combined. It is also larger than New York city's Central Park. Under the golden sun, a seed of curiosity began to take root. As fate would have it, on that very day when the fair graced the town with its presence, a dear friend and I found ourselves drawn to the mystic allure of palm readers. Little did I know this would be my first foray into the world of divination, leading me to many more encounters in the years to come. Before we entered the caravan, my friend and I made a solemn vow to listen to each other's readings, lest any magical insights be missed. Through the vibrant array of caravans, their metallic sheen reflecting the sun's rays, Vicki and I scoured the market for the perfect abode. Yet fate had other plans as we stumbled upon a dilapidated caravan with smudged silver and tarnished brass. A pungent odour emanated from within as we approached, and our apprehension grew as we spotted two ladies inside. One sat hunched over the table, a cigarette in one hand and a cup of tea in the other, while the other lay motionless on the small bed in the corner, leaving us unsure whether she was even alive. As we sat down, the old lady began talking to a deck of cards, narrating tales of past and future events with an eerie accuracy that left us spellbound.

In the years that followed, I would often recall this chance encounter with Vicki, awed by the lady's prophetic abilities as her predictions happened. As I stood before the mystic, she spoke of omens that foretold of my future. She revealed to me that my blood would require vigilance and that the path ahead would lead me to distant lands. Her words echoed with a promise of an interview awaiting me, assuring me that the job was already mine. As I emerged from the mystical realm, the weight of her revelations kept me in a trance, and I remained silent until we reached the familiar path leading back home.

As the sun dipped below the horizon on a Friday evening, the Hexham Courant arrived, and I found myself at home. It was then that my mother informed me of a new opening for a junior travel consultant position in Hexham. My intuition stirred within me, for I knew this was the job the palm reader had foretold. Though my mother doubted the mystic's claims, I kept it to myself. The day of the interview was unremarkable, and I drove to Hexham without a hint of unease. As I sat across from the owner of the shop, it felt as though we were old friends, reunited at last. She offered to sponsor my education, allowing me to gain the necessary qualifications for a career in the travel industry. The fates had aligned, and I knew that this was my destiny. For three cycles of the seasons, I found myself within the halls of the travel agents. The first year was the most challenging for me, as I was eager to sink my teeth into new experiences. Yet as I was once again the junior, my days were consumed with brewing coffee and mundane tasks. It was a humbling experience for me, having already spent two years as an apprentice. In hindsight, it granted me a glimpse into an enthralling realm. Travelling to exotic destinations was only one part of the job. We also attended trade shows in Newcastle upon Tyne, where we danced the night away until the wee hours, knowing that we would soon be back at work. The following day would be spent reminiscing about the previous night's antics. If there was a birthday or any other excuse for a girly get-together, it was sure to be both late and messy, with copious amounts of alcohol consumed.

The travel agent's invitation sparked the beginning of my first all-girls adventure. After pooling our resources, we secured a week's stay in Rhodes, a jewel of an island nestled in the embrace of Greece's Aegean Sea. The only caveat was that we would not know where we would be staying until the day of our arrival. As fate would have it, we were granted a breathtaking view of Lindros, a village steeped in history and myth, crowned by an acropolis that loomed above us majestically. Our self-catering apartment became our sanctuary for the week, granting us the perfect base to explore and discover the wonders of Rhodes.

With an insatiable thirst for history, one can unearth a treasure trove of cultural heritage, replete with tales of ancient times. As you traverse the path that winds from the airport to Lindos, the landscape unfolds like a picturesque canvas, with verdant orchards and farmers tending to their land. Enchanting vistas greet you as the dazzling white abodes and the glistening shoreline caress the clear waters. The narrow-cobbled streets, intertwined with shops and residential houses, lead to a petite supermarket that spills its wares in a charming display. Adventurers may choose to ascend the acropolis on a donkey ride or bravely trek the path themselves, basking in the breathtaking views that await. Although Lindos may not have been the hotspot for travellers in the late '80s, it was a haven for newlyweds and couples, beckoning them towards unforgettable journeys through the ages. Let me take you on a wild adventure into my travels through the wondrous world of tourism.

The misty hills of Co. Durham loomed as I began my quest to unlock the secrets of travel agents. The training curriculum was a maze of information, leading me to the final challenge of end-of-year exams. Two routes emerged: the general section, loaded with juicy details on package vacations, and the air travel manual, a treasure trove of knowledge on crafting customized itineraries in areas from far-flung lands to local skies. I spent an incredibly challenging but exciting time in both the travel agent and the college; in the three years that followed, I progressed through many hurdles of training and exams.

CHAPTER 8

Back in 1992, when I was just a wee twenty-year-old, my folks made a bold decision. They ditched the pub business and went after their lifelong passions. Keeping field sport and game was in our family DNA for at least two generations, and my dad was ready to carry that torch. As for my mum, she was itching to master her green fingers, and both were ready for some serious R&R.

The year I lived with my grandparents was an absolute blast! When I was not snoozing, I was working my socks off at the travel agent or celebrating with friends. If you were not chasing me down winding roads in my Citroën 2CV, you would find me exploring the latest nightlife hotspots. Edinburgh was a regular haunt, and thanks to my job rewards, we would always stay in the fanciest hotels and hangouts. Endless memories! Picture this: I am on the phone with my folks, chatting casually, when my mum drops, "Hey, there's a job going in Carlisle for a travel agent. Interested?" My first reaction? Meh. I was wrapped up in my cosy job up in Hexham, where customers were treated like royalty. But I decided to check it out anyway. Fast forward to a late-night interview in which we were chatting casually about their company history and work style. Just as I was about to say goodbye, the boss asked me when I could start! I had bagged myself a second travel job, and it felt as if the stars were aligning. This was my true calling!

In the heart of the Scottish borders lies the charming town of Langholm. Once a bustling hub for textiles and thievery, it is now a hub for handcrafted figurines that locals take immense pride in. This spirit of pride runs deep in the town, with generations upon generations following in their ancestors' footsteps. One of the town's biggest events is the Common Riding, held on the last Friday of July. The town comes alive with the sound of galloping horses, brass bands, and bagpipes, and the crowning of the cornet, who leads the charge. It is a remarkable sight and attracts visitors from all corners of the UK. But the fun does not stop there; the preceding days are filled with thrilling ride-outs through the neighbouring countryside. So, saddle up and join in on the fun! Picture this: a grand parade of people, horses, and bands, all following the enchanting cornet through the town. The horses neigh in history-filled glory as they are led towards the hills, away from the parade. The rest of the day is spent on the nearby common land, where Scottish dancers and horses race to the finish line. It is a day on which both locals and visitors unite, catching up on the last twelve months of missed memories. And let us not forget about the pubs! Open from 6.00 a.m. on Friday morning, they keep the drinks flowing until the wee hours of the morning. Surprisingly, despite the long hours of merrymaking, the town has never seen any trouble, likely owing to either the friendly locals or the watchful eye of the constabulary. Whatever the secret ingredient, this traditional local event remains a beloved part of the town's history.

In the lead-up to the Common Riding event, I invited a couple of buds to Langholm, hoping to soak up the town's pre-festival vibes. With only a handful of pubs to choose from, we planned our night out to a T. And boy, was it a wild ride! The locals were buzzing with curiosity about us out-of-towners, and the drinks were flowing like a river. Soon enough, we were belting out Scottish tunes like nobody's business. As we stumbled out of the pubs, giggling and holding each other up, I could not help but chuckle at being the only sober one in a group of rowdy ladies. Picture this: We were whizzing down the road from Langholm, all squeezed into a Citroën 2CV. The twists and turns were crazier than a carnival ride, but we made it out alive—or so we thought. Suddenly a blazing electric-blue light show appeared in the rear-view mirror, making it seem as if the entire police force was hot on our heels. Heart racing, knees knocking, we pulled over into the nearest lay-by. What did we do wrong? No idea. As the officer approached us, we were listening carefully, eager to hear what the deal was. But he had a different idea. "Out of the car," he commanded, motioning for us to stand beside his colleague. As I handed over my driving licence, the officer had a few curious questions about my whereabouts. I could not believe it when my friends climbed from the backseat, confirming my story about a night out in Langholm after picking them up in Hexham. The whole squad even tried on the police officers' hats and goofed around with the CB radio to call in to headquarters. It was a hilarious moment that we will never forget, and after they checked our info, we were cleared to hit the road again.

That unexpected in-person meeting was just the beginning of my run-ins with the law in Dumfries and Galloway. I decided to follow in my grandad's footsteps and become a special constable. After my acceptance, I spent weeks reporting to headquarters in Dumfries, eagerly awaiting my crisp new uniform. Let me take you on a fashion trip back in time! Imagine a black skirt, tickling just below the knee, with fine wool fabric and a subtle flare. Tucked into it was a white shirt, adorned with extra buttonholes on the shoulders to attach lapels when it was too hot for a jacket. A tunic, sporting four large silver buttons down the front, was made from the same fine wool material. Winter months were no match for the sturdy jacket, but it was a bit much for the summer. To round off the look, black flat shoes and tights were necessary. These days, the navy woollen jumper and black trousers have taken over the police fashion scene, but we will never forget the good old days of the skirt-and-tunic combo! A brand-new adventure was unfolding before my eyes, complete with fresh faces to call friends.

For a whopping thirteen years, I was part of the special constabulary, tackling everything from accidents to sudden deaths. Every day was a chance to learn something new, a chance to explore. In the beginning, I was still working full-time at a travel agency, but as soon as I got home, I would slip into my uniform and join the force. Looking back, I do not recall being tired or drained, but I do remember looking a little too pale for comfort. I was so swept up in my job and hobbies that I completely forgot to take care of numero uno—that is, me! Following a gruelling work schedule, I had been pushing myself to the limit for months. But my body was waving the white flag, and I knew something had to give. So, I switched things up and limited my work to weekends only. But my body had already taken a hit. One day while I was busy hustling, my leg slipped, and I pulled some muscles. But, like a trooper, I ignored the pain and kept going—that is until the pain grew to be too much. It began to concentrate on my calf muscle, and every time I tried to walk, it felt as if a dagger were stabbing me. I tried every trick in the book to ease the pain, but nothing worked. Finally, I went to the doctor, who took one look at my leg and sent me straight to the hospital in Carlisle.

It was a typical day when I heard the term "DVT" for the first time. I had no clue what it meant, unlike today, when you hear stories of travellers having issues with blood flow in their legs. When I first landed in hospital, the doctor must have thought I was from another planet, given my blasé attitude. After donning gorgeous white stockings and enduring a week of bed rest, the real fun began. Nurse after nurse tried to insert a cannula into the back of my hand, but my deep and jiggly veins would not cooperate. It was a tiny pink cannula, usually reserved for infants, which saved the day. From that point on, I was known for my tricky veins and my DVT battle. Picture this: a tiny cassette-like machine was wired to a cannula, which was jabbed into my vein. The machine's job was to pump heparin into my bloodstream at regular intervals. Sounds harmless, right? Except heparin is also known as rat poison! Yes, that is right, the same stuff that makes rats bleed to death. I was a curious cat during my hospital stay, and I asked a gazillion questions about my circulatory system. Why was I struck with this weird condition that usually hit people who are overweight or heavy smokers? I did not fit into either of those categories! Sadly, the doctors did not have a clear answer, but it got me hooked on all things blood and body. When I was not flipping through magazines, I was glued to TV shows that promised the next big cure. Unfortunately, there were no Google searches back in the day! Upon my return home, I was ordered to continue taking warfarin until notified otherwise.

The following weeks passed quickly, and no additional blood clots were detected, leading to the conclusion that they may have been stress-induced. Consequently, the medication was discontinued a few months later. While continuing to work in both the travel agency and police station, I reduced my weekend work hours.

CHAPTER 9

The year 1993 holds a special place in my heart, with moments of mirth and a milestone of turning twenty-one. As the gentle breeze of spring wafted, I felt the promise of a fresh start, with a job that kindled my passion and colleagues who inspired me. Life had already gifted me invaluable lessons, yet I yearned for more, eager to unravel the mysteries of the world. And so, my wanderlust ignited, and I set my sights on exploring distant lands. As fate would have it, my next adventure was a celebratory voyage to Cyprus, with a dear friend by my side, spanning two weeks of joy and wonder. As we dreamed of traversing the globe, our hearts alight with wanderlust, the sands of fate beckoned us towards the isle of Cyprus. This was a chance for us to immerse ourselves in the rich tapestry of its culture and tread the paths of its people, and for me to hone my skills behind the bar. Yet coins held a mystical power over our plans, and the quest to secure work became our priority. We scoured every nook and cranny, from hotels to garages, in search of opportunity, but the same answers echoed through the winds of destiny: "Not at this time" or "Leave your details." A singular offer emerged to distribute promotion cards on the streets, but we shared a laugh, for our aspirations soared far beyond such endeavours. And so we returned to the serenity of the pool, basking in the warmth of the sun's embrace, and dreaming of the enchantments yet to come. As the seasons shifted from the vibrant bloom of spring to the languid days of summer, our minds were brimming with ideas, yet no date was set for our next adventure. In September, we tried to satiate our wanderlust with a brief sojourn to Cyprus, but in hindsight, it only left us yearning for more. The cosmos whispered a different plan, or perhaps the time for travel was not ripe. Regardless, we knew that greater magic awaited us on the horizon.

The whims of fate are a curious game, yet sometimes one must seek the key to unlock its mysteries. My fascination with palm readers and mediums persisted through the ages, and I sought their counsel for many moons. Some prophesied that I would journey to distant lands, while others warned me of the fragility of my joints. One mystic even foretold that I would wed and bear two children—a memory that still tickles my soul to this day. However, as time passed, I became wary of charlatans who sought to pry into the depths of my being, luring me with the promise of divine revelations. But through the guidance of trusted friends, I found my way to those who held the gift of true divination, and their wisdom shone like a beacon in the night. As much as I believed the messages, I gave nothing away. If these people had such a gift, there would be no reason for them to ask various questions. One of those days for me to attend a palmist had arrived again, as I had no idea what line I should follow. My heart was telling me to travel the world, while my head telling me to wait a little while and continue with both the travel agent and my police work.

CHAPTER 10

Enchanted by the tales woven by these soothsayers, I listened anxiously yet revealed naught of my thoughts. "Can they truly read the threads of fate," I wondered, "or are they mere charlatans seeking clues through queries?" As the fates would have it, I found myself drawn to seek the wisdom of a palmist once more. Perchance, my destiny lay in traversing the globe, beckoned by the siren call of wanderlust. Yet my logical mind urged patience and continuing weaving threads with both the travel agency and the guardians of justice. The path ahead, shrouded in mystery, awaited the touch of magic to reveal its secrets. The future, a tapestry of fate, hung heavy in the hands of the palmist. At first, the tryst I arranged with my trusted soothsayer seemed destined for success. But, as if woven by the strands of destiny, the threads began to unravel. Appointments with my guide were postponed without cause, and whispers of a greater force danced in my mind. Strange happenings began to surround me as if the ether itself sought to thwart my quest for knowledge. The phone line would falter, and I could barely reach out to my seer before the connection was lost, leaving me stranded in a world without answers.

As the stars danced in their cosmic rhythm, an unwelcome guest arrived at my doorstep—pain that wracked my joints and dampened my spirit. In my quest for solace, I reached out for the palmist's touch, but to no avail. Instead, I found myself reaching out to the healers of the land, seeking refuge from the agony. And so, I journeyed to the local doctor, who, with eyes of wisdom, took my blood and prescribed magical potions to soothe my aches. Yet the palmist's touch eluded me that year, and with a heavy heart, I let go of the quest. Did I accidentally stumble upon a secret conversation? Were there hushed whispers meant to be kept concealed? I had an epiphany when I stumbled upon a wise saying in a book: "What's meant to be will always find a way." As a woman, I trust my gut instinct, which feels like a superpower. The more you tune in to it, the clearer it becomes. This philosophy has fascinated me for years, and I still live by it. When you have an unquenchable desire in your heart and it feels like a perfect fit, my advice is to take the plunge and explore it. You never know where your path may lead unless you take that first step!

Diane hit the road, driving lorries across Europe though I was bewitched by their words, my stoic facade remained unbroken. I could not fathom how those blessed with a mystical talent had to resort to inquiries to peel the layers of my soul. And yet the calling of destiny beckoned me to a palmist, for my wandering spirit needed a guiding star. Should I heed the whispers of my heart and set sail on adventures across the world? Or should I stay and tend to the fields of my labour, aiding both the travel agent and the guardians of the law? The answer, like a riddle of fate, eluded me. So, I took this advice and went full throttle. I kissed my travel agent's job goodbye and booked a one-way ticket to Australia. I thought my ex-girlfriend was joining me, but— surprise, surprise—it was a new boyfriend! We were in for the long haul, with him taking a three-month sabbatical down under with me. Let us just say it was a wild ride of difficulties! No itinerary, no problem! We were like two explorers craving a blank slate of adventure, our only compass being wanderlust. Our journey kicked off with a trip from Newcastle to Amsterdam, followed by a pit stop in Bangkok before finally landing in Sydney. Despite my knees, elbows, and wrists causing havoc in the weeks leading up to our departure, the flight was smoother than expected, and the pain was just a tiny bump in the journey. Bring on the adventure! I was living the dream with my eyes wide open, never once thinking that the flight could be a threat or make my old DVT worries come back to haunt me.

After reaching our destination, I reunited with some dear friends from my Kielder days. Amongst them was Christo, who had been blind since birth. He now resided in a cosy suburb called Five Docks, a quick twenty-minute ferry ride away from the bustling Sydney centre, with his trusty sidekick Kay, his guide dog. Chris and Jane had flown the coop to Australia in the sixties, yet they still managed to pop back to the UK for occasional visits. Their nest was perched in the breathtaking Blue Mountains region, where they played host like kings and queens. They took us on a wild tour of Sydney's sparkling sights and nearby national parks—the kind of stuff that would make David Attenborough blush.

I grew up in the countryside, so I was not sure how a bustling city like Sydney would treat me, but boy was I in for a surprise! The bridge by day and night whisked me right back to our wild nights in Newcastle upon Tyne, where we would sip chardonnay and spill all the tea with friends. But the real jaw-dropper was the city's transport system, especially the boats zipping people around the suburbs. It is like the city's own water taxi service, and I found it simply incredible. Imagine boats the size of our trusty tourist ferries back home, but these let you hop on and off around the city! In the morning, I could spend hours taking in the sights and sounds as people from all over the world bustled to work with bags under their arms, tickets at the ready, their faces sporting a slightly shiny complexion from the three-inch layer of sunblock they applied an hour prior. It was like watching a film come to life!

Why is it that when us "pommies" venture off to foreign lands, we act like we are the know-it-alls of the town? Back in 1993, we were still snoozing on the sun-protection train while the Aussies were miles ahead. They slathered on SPF 50 every couple of hours and even went all-out with full-on sun-blocking masks that made them look like their Aboriginal ancestors! Guess we will have to take notes from the wise Aussies next time we hit the beach.

Picture this: a leisurely stroll on Bondi Beach on an ordinary day. We felt chilled and had our arms and legs tucked away, forgetting the sunscreen we had slapped on six hours before. Oh boy, did we pay the price! The next two days were a painful lesson in how not to do sunscreen. During the initial three weeks of the heatwave, it did provide some relief to my aches and pains, which had been gradually intensifying. Previously, I would spend restless nights tossing and turning because of the discomfort, often resorting to a hot bath to alleviate the pain concentrated around my joints.

As the weeks rolled by, we journeyed to breathtaking destinations. We went as far as Canberra down south, the Hunter Valley wine region, and the cherry on top—the spellbinding Blue Mountains. We chose a rental car as our trusty steed, and boy, did it never let us down! We even turned the car bonnet into a clothesline one day while I navigated with my pioneering map-reading skills, leading to a fiery debate.

As a seasoned navigator of Kielder Forest, I thought getting around in Australia would be a breeze. After all, I am a woman who knows her way around! But I will admit I had to fess up to turning the map around to match my direction. I mean, it just made sense in my female brain, right? Well, that small confession turned into a full-blown battle of the voices. We got out of the car, and our shouting match echoed through the air. The map was flipped, then flipped again, and then spun around like a yo-yo. In the end, we ended up back in the car, laughing about our little navigation tussle. Just hear me out; we were in the Southern Hemisphere, where even the water drains in the opposite direction! I mean, what chance did I have? Despite the debate heating up, we had a blast and created memories that will stick with us forever.

As time passed, my aches turned into monster pains, making some days extra unbearable for both of us. My knees and elbows became stubborn, refusing to bend smoothly as they used to. It was as if someone stole the oil that kept everything in check! To make things worse, the joints turned an angry red, adding another layer of worry. It was a real bummer that we had to cut our trip short and board the next flight back to the UK. On top of that, my pain made me an absolute grumpster to be around, and to make matters worse, I had to head straight to the doctor's office. It was like running a marathon and being stopped in your tracks by an invisible force. The frustration was real! It was just like the cartoons we all love, where the characters see stars after a whack on the head, like Tom and Jerry or the Road Runner!

The relationship with my boyfriend sadly ended upon our return to the UK, due to many side effects caused by the medication.

Additional tests were conducted, but no conclusive explanation was found for my condition. There were speculations about a potential virus, but no definitive diagnosis was made. Over time, the pain would intermittently subside for a few weeks, only to resurface with heightened intensity. On certain occasions, the redness around a joint would escalate, appearing akin to a burn or an allergic reaction.

CHAPTER 11

Some months after returning from my trip to Australia, I had an unexpected encounter with my former travel agent manager. He informed me that they were understaffed and inquired as to whether I could assist them. I readily accepted the offer and commenced work at the Carlisle office the following week. They were aware of my previous joint pain issues and provided me with time off to attend medical appointments and clinics for further evaluations. I frequently experienced sudden shifts from being an active twenty-one-year-old to being incapacitated because of the pain. These unpredictable swings led to self-doubt, and it was challenging for others to comprehend the gravity of the situation. Consequently, I would hear comments such as "There doesn't appear to be anything wrong with her today" or "She looks fit and healthy to me; it must be all in her head." While it was frustrating to hear these statements, I tried my best to remain composed and withhold my reaction. On some days, I would consider the possibility that everyone else was right and it was all just my imagination. But then, on other days, I would be hit with such excruciating pain that I would crumple to the ground, the thoughts of doubt erased from my mind. The flare-ups showed no pattern, no rhyme or reason, and it seemed as though no one was listening to me. I started to feel as if I were dealing with a mysterious, unheard-of disease.

After the local doctor collected numerous bottles of blood samples, a range of tests were conducted, including for AIDS, multiple sclerosis, and other autoimmune diseases. Despite these efforts, a definitive diagnosis could not be established, and I was subsequently referred to a rheumatologist. After the initial assessment by the consultant, a series of tests were ordered to evaluate my skeletal system. These tests included

X-rays and scans, as well as procedures involving the introduction of dyes into my bloodstream to locate blockages. Additionally, certain joints were manipulated to identify any pain or discomfort during movement. I attended all my appointments at the hospital without a single wince or grimace, even though my body was aching with stiffness and pain. It was a frustrating experience, as I could not provide any clues to the healthcare providers about what I was going through. It was as though no one was buying my story. I tried to power through work for four months before waving the white flag and taking a three-year break. It was like running a marathon on one leg!

Honestly, I had nothing but admiration for the medical team who helped me along the way. The term "psychosomatic" has a negative connotation, often associated with the belief that physical symptoms are solely a result of one's mental state. This interpretation can be wearisome, particularly when medical tests show no definitive diagnosis. Pain, in all its forms, is a shared experience. Be it a sports injury, menstrual cramps, childbirth, or a migraine, many of us have endured some level of physical discomfort. Pain thresholds vary from person to person, regardless of the degree of pain. Personally, I consider my pain threshold to be high. However, when speaking with others about pain, it is common to hear them express how it can drive them to despair. Regrettably, this is precisely where I found myself at this moment.

My morning routine often involved taking painkillers or trying the latest remedy that promised to provide a quick cure. I was caught up in the trend of constantly scouting health magazines for the next best medicine or treatment to alleviate the debilitating discomfort, including aloe vera juice, massage creams, sprays, and herbal remedies. Nothing would lift the discomfort, and I would have to resort to my only remedy of having a red-hot bath and eventually retiring to my bed. Sometimes I would just lie in bed, not wanting to move in case the motion would activate feelings like a screwdriver being forced into my joints and then twisted. Lying there like a statue, I could hear my heart drumming against my bones, making me wonder what was cooking inside my body. I was given some painkillers, which did the trick, but boy, did they make me feel like a hot air balloon! I only took them before bedtime, and nope, I did not have a sip of alcohol. The impact was mind-blowing! I was not sure whether I wanted to stick with it, but these pills had me feeling like a puppet with no strings attached. Let us just say that my memories were a little hazy after taking them.

I was hooked on learning about the side effects of drugs, and I was devouring leaflets and books to understand how they worked and their impact on the body, both in the short and long terms. During my commute to a clinic appointment one morning, I experienced the debilitating effects of my pain, which could strike without warning and render me immobile. Despite my having made the twenty-five-minute journey to the travel agent in Carlisle numerous times over the past year, this instance highlighted the unpredictable nature of my condition. At the break of dawn, I made a conscious decision to leave my home earlier than usual. The dull, persistent pain that had plagued me in recent days had subsided, holding to the pattern observed on days I had scheduled clinic appointments. Imagine this: you are cruising down a curvy road, eyes peeled for speedy animals. It is an early-morning drive that will make your adrenalin pump! Suddenly you spot a small town and a pedestrian crossing with buttons galore, guaranteed to make any kid's day. But wait! Who is this? Two sharp young adults just strutted their stuff and pressed those buttons as if it were nothing! As the pedestrian crossing light turned green, I proceeded cautiously, maintaining a speed of thirty miles per hour. I then observed two young adults in the middle of the road, causing me to tense up and experience intense pain in both my legs. Despite my attempts to evade them, I was unable to move as I approached them. To alert them of my presence, I honked the horn located in the centre of the steering wheel. The two men quickly fled to the other side of the road with barely inches to spare. My only option was to bring the car to a halt as quickly as possible. With great force, I pulled the handbrake and hit the brakes, causing the car to screech to a stop with the smell of burning rubber lingering in the air.

I was overwhelmed with shock. Tears streamed down my face while my legs shook uncontrollably. Two young men hurried over to inspect the situation, relieved that the potential for an accident had been averted. Initially I found myself speechless, but eventually I opened about my past experiences. My companions listened attentively and kindly offered me a cup of locally purchased tea to comfort me. Although I do not remember much about the trip to and from the clinic that day, I realize now that it was a pivotal moment in my medical history. The events of that day remain hazy, though the morning trauma is still fresh in my mind.

Seated in the consultation room, the doctor and nurse proceeded to assess the range of motion in my joints, which had been causing immense discomfort. During the appointment, the results of my blood tests from the previous visit were disclosed. As the appointment ended, the doctor perused my medical notes, sat back in his chair, and, with a pen poised over his mouth, uttered the words, "We believe we've identified the root of your troubles. You have been diagnosed with systemic lupus erythematosus, or SLE for short." Receiving such information can be overwhelming, disorienting, and can leave one feeling helpless. I recall how my senses seemed to betray me, rendering me speechless and unable to concentrate. The situation was further compounded by the abrupt termination of the appointment. I was left to my own devices, with only a vague assurance of receiving assistance from a nurse at the reception. Upon my exiting the room, the nurse assisted me to the desk, where she informed me that there was no information available regarding my condition and she was unclear about lupus. Despite feeling overwhelmed, I managed to make it home later that afternoon. The nurse's words kept playing in my mind, leading me to speculate that it was not as severe as I initially assumed. However, I also felt that the lack of information available might also suggest an error or a less serious condition.

As soon as I stepped through the front door, the name of my diagnosis vanished like a magician's rabbit. When I tried to explain the morning's appointment to my folks, I was as lost as they were. So we just kept trucking along, clueless but determined. During a visit from a friend of mine, Sharon, who had recently joined the Specials, we conversed over coffee. As we discussed my last medical appointment, I struggled to recall the exact name of my illness, recollecting only some of the letters. I suggested it might be LES, ESL, or SLE, but I could not be certain. Sharon, a full-time nurse at a local hospital, offered to return with some medical books to help us investigate further. Sharon returned as promised but, unfortunately, empty-handed. During our conversation, we failed to find any leads regarding my illness.

As time went by, I started to wonder whether she had forgotten about it. However, I continued talking, and eventually I inquired whether she'd had any luck finding information about my condition. Sharon confirmed that she had, but the available books contained information dating back to the 1950s and were not up to date. Months later, Sharon revealed that the books she had consulted indicated that not much was known about the illness, which often resulted in fatalities. Lupus can manifest in several ways, and unfortunately some individuals may go undiagnosed for months or even years. Owing to the extensive range of symptoms associated with the disease, it is possible for diagnosis to be overlooked or missed.

Some of the symptoms associated with systemic lupus erythematosus are as follows:

- joint and muscle aches and pains
- permanent rash over cheeks
- extreme fatigue and weakness
- increased risk of miscarriage
- rashes from sunlight and UV light
- flu-like symptoms.
- night sweats
- weight gain or loss.
- inflammation of the tissues covering internal organs, with associated chest and/or abdominal pain
- seizures, mental illness, or other cerebral problems
- headaches, migraine
- kidney problems
- oral and nasal ulcers
- hair loss
- depression
- haematological disorders including anaemia.

- swollen glands
- poor blood circulation, causing the tips of fingers and toes to turn white and then blue on exposure to cold (Raynaud's phenomenon)

Symptoms of this illness can vary from person to person. While some may experience only one or two symptoms, others may suffer from the complete list. In my case, symptoms appeared one after the other.

A suitable analogy to understand this illness is the immune system of a body under attack by a virus or bacteria failing to perform its primary function and, instead of combating the invaders, turning on the body's cells and organs, causing harm.

Several weeks had transpired since my previous appointment, where I received a diagnosis for my illness. I spent numerous days and nights confined to bed, attempting to manage the pain and alleviate the discomfort, which was intensifying with each passing day. Even when I managed to get out of bed, I remained vigilant, mindful of any movements that could potentially trigger my symptoms. There are moments when I wished only my knees were impacted, which would have enabled me to carry out daily tasks, such as boiling water and lifting a mug of coffee using my hands. As time progressed, I began to listen to my body, learning which actions are suitable and which are not. However, I must admit I struggled with frustration and anger, which is not very ladylike. I vividly recall a time when I experienced excruciating pain in my fingers, wrists, and arms, rendering me unable to open the fridge door. The overwhelming feelings of frustration and helplessness began to consume me and I could not help but question why I was the one going through such agony. As tears streamed down my face and anger surged through my body, I impulsively kicked the fridge door with my booted foot, causing it to buckle and crack beneath the handle.

After my outburst, I found myself collapsed on the floor, overwhelmed by pain and discomfort, and in tears. The ensuing days were filled with frustration and disappointment, with the uncertainty of my life's direction overshadowing the enjoyable moments spent in the garden at our Langholm residence. The rented house in Langholm was an employment reward that came with my father's new position as a gamekeeper. It was located just outside the town of Langholm, surrounded by forest land and fields; our only neighbours were a retired couple who had lived both in around the town all their lives. It brought back memories of my earlier days in the estate cottage; even the house had similar quirky features, such as the exceedingly small kitchen and bedrooms crammed into the roof space. The garden was huge—a good twenty or so metres long, leading away from the house and into the wooded area at the bottom. The main garden area was covered in grass, with a line of conifers shading the stony path that led to the garden shed. Behind the conifers was an area where the previous occupiers had planted fruit bushes. There were many outbuildings surrounding the house, which lodged garden tools, logs, coal, horse feed, tack, and Wellington boots. We even allocated one of the larger sheds as a stable for my mother's horse.

CHAPTER 12

We had four dogs, all housed outside in their own kennel, two of which belonged to my father and were used as part of his occupation as a gamekeeper. Working Labradors have a lovely nature but have only one expert, that being my father. They had worked hard during the winter months and now were enjoying the warm summer days of 1994. The third dog, Hess, was our resident guard dog from our days in the Red Lion, a beautiful German shepherd whose bark was louder than his bite. He was a beautiful black and tan colour. Our fourth dog was my favourite; this was Hess's daughter Heather. The only difference between the two of them was that she was long haired and he had a smooth coat. Heather was a wonderfully soft-natured dog who would never leave my side. She would watch me and listen to my every command—more so if I were having a poor day on my legs. The days were sometimes exceptionally long as I just sat in the garden with Heather, trying to make sense of what was happening to me.

On one afternoon that summer, I had spent time in the garden, soaking up as much sun as I could before returning indoors for lunch; along with hot baths, the sun also injected some warmth into my bones. My appetite had not been the best for a few weeks, and my weight loss was beginning to show. Tea and toast were to be my daily diet, with the possible cravings for grapes, strawberries, and bananas. During my lunch, I started to feel unwell, so I retired to my bed. Shortly afterwards, my grandparents arrived, and I could hear their voices from upstairs. It must not have been long before I fell asleep again. Before my grandparents left that afternoon, my grandfather came up to check on me and was also keen for me to try his newly brewed elderflower wine. As I came to, I could not manage to lift my head to greet him.

The more I tried, the more pain echoed through me. On witnessing this, my parents were asked to come and check on me. My parents had never experienced me in this corpse-like state, so without further action the doctor was called.

Within a brief time, the doctor was at my bedside, looked into my eyes, checked my wrists and elbows, and then asked whether an ambulance could be called straight away. The journey that followed was a blur for me, but my parents informed me later that night that it was a bit of déjà vu for them, with history repeating itself from years earlier. I was admitted to the city hospital in Carlisle that afternoon, which is now no longer there. I was stretchered in through the large sandstone pillars and onwards to a nurse's desk, where the sister took the envelope on which the doctor had written down a few of my relevant and important medical notes.

The hospital had that smell of disinfectant again, together with the long, straight corridors. From what I recall, the largest ward was directly in front of me, with about twelve beds near an oblong table in the centre that was covered with folders. I never got any closer to that ward. Instead, I was to be placed in a small six-bed ward situated just off the long corridor. Once I arrived at my bed, which was situated by the window, I asked whether I could manoeuvre myself, as any additional help seemed to add to and cause further pain. While I was lying in bed, the nurses asked me various questions regarding my date of birth, next of kin, and so forth while they waited for my medical notes to arrive from the other main hospital in Carlisle, the Infirmary. When they did eventually arrive, I am sure they all would have been heading for their previous study books, as everyone kept asking me questions about SLE! "Where did you get it from? How did you get it? How long have you had it?" The questions went on and on. One even went on to say, "Try not to worry too much." I think that if I'd had the strength, I would have slapped her. I was told that if I needed anything, I could press the buzzer, which was located next to my bed.

I suppose it was through a mixture of sheer determination and having little or no patience that I decided try to venture to the toilets alone—not a clever move when your legs have a mind of their own and you are not sure where you are headed. The corridor walls were lined with a wooden railing that ran from one end of the ward to the other. As I huffed and puffed myself out of bed, I had made it to the railings. Just as I reached out to take another step, my knees give way without warning, and I collapsed in a heap on the icy cold floor. As the nurses came running, one of them took one look at me and told me to get up and stop wasting their time with silly little pains. "Legs just do not stop working; get up, girl." From that day onwards, those words would never leave me.

I needed to find out more about this illness—not only for myself but for others too, including nurses and patients going through the same experience. I spent about a week in that hospital, having additional tests done on both blood and joints. Further tests included urine tests, which were to open a new chapter in the illness. The urine test was one test which, up until that point, had never been asked for, so when it was discovered that there was blood present in my urine, it set alarm bells ringing with both the medical staff and me. At this point, I asked a nurse what this really meant, her answer came as a shock. She replied with a detailed account about how my kidneys might not be working correctly. The contamination in my urine could be detected only with a medically prepared dipstick; as well as blood they could also evaluate for protein, glucose, and ketones.

That night I was to be transferred to the Infirmary for further examination. The Infirmary, in comparison to the City Hospital, was massive. The corridors and door handles seemed so much newer than previously, and complete with people, doctors, and nurses everywhere, it was a hive of activity. There were a couple of incredibly old, listed buildings located right in the heart of the hospital grounds, additional buildings comprising the pathology department and portacabins used for physiotherapy. The ward had six beds. As in the city hospital, there were small rooms that led off the main corridor. These rooms, I later discovered, were isolation rooms. Any seriously ill patients would have occupied them. The nurses on this ward were some of nicest I had ever met, and this was the first time anyone other than my family started to understand what pain and discomfort I was going through. I often asked whether they had come across this illness before. Some answered with an honest no but said they would investigate to find out more, and some said that they had heard the word "lupus" while training but did not know much about the condition.

It was during this time in the infirmary that the nurses helped me locate national organizations regarding my ailments. The two main addresses I had been given were those of Lupus UK and Versus Arthritis. These proved to be a lifeline for so many questions and the advice I longed for. At this time as well, we were still about four or five years away from the Internet and email, so everything took an age to arrive in the post. I was soon receiving leaflets informing me of advice on treatment, up-to-date drug therapy, and people offering help and support.

The ward was very busy with many people arriving or leaving once they had recovered. During my six-week stay in that ward, I made a huge number of friends and shared an overwhelming account of patients' backgrounds, it was so therapeutic to hear of other people's ailments that I would end up consoling patients when times became too much for them. It would really make me think that it was not particularly bad in my life and that there were people a lot worse off than I.

Over the next few days, the pain did subside with the help of medication, together with anti-inflammatory painkillers and prednisolone steroids. At first I was not sure whether it had been the combination of all the medication, but what they had prescribed had certainly given me a new lease of life. My legs started to work again and were beginning to feel as if they belonged to me and not a disabled old woman with twisted bones. As the steroids started to get into my system, I started to notice an increase in movement within my joints and changes in my appetite. This also improved, and soon I became a healthier weight. In the early days, I would have classed these drugs as my best friend, but soon additional problems were to raise their ugly heads.

Within a week of taking the steroids, I was forced to return to my hospital bed with debilitating migraines. This was an all-singing, all-dancing, flashing lights affair that sent me hiding under the covers, not wanting to talk to anybody about anything. These migraines went on for four days before the nurses managed to relocate me to one of the side rooms. These rooms were complete with a chair, the hospital bed, and a sink in the corner for washing. There were two large windows behind the bed that opened onto the gardens in front of the listed buildings. I lay in my semi-conscious state for four days. I even remember telling the cleaner to leave before I placed the mop somewhere other than in in her bucket! My head did not seem to belong to me, my stomach ached from vomiting, and now I was getting ill-tempered. It did not matter how nice those nurses were; I could not get away from this pain and from feeling out of control. During that week, I had all kinds of specialists visiting my bedside. Both neurological professionals and physiotherapists offered their own conclusions even after brain scans and CAT scans were performed, but still no explanation was given. It was decided to change some of my painkillers around, and additional new ones were tried.

Whatever they did at this point, my headaches, sickness, and pain eased and I started to come round to being myself again. I later found out that they had increased the steroids, which were again proving to be the wonder drug. As the weeks progressed, all my joint pain subsided together with the headaches. My appetite increased to such an extent that I would never feel full after a meal and would ask whether the nurses or visiting family or friends would bring further snacks into the hospital for me. My weight increased by over a stone within those few weeks. As any woman will tell you, it is easy to snack on the sweet things in life, like your favourite piece of milk chocolate or that temping bowl of trifle but trying to deny them is much harder.

I started to see the side effects that these steroids were having on my weight. I also noticed the moon-like face appearing in the mirror. These are common side effects of these drugs. I hated looking into the mirror in the mornings and seeing this face that, quite frankly, was not me. I was asking myself what more I must deal with, not content with the pains, which were less severe now—although I looked like a person who had been blown up into a woman with an obsession to eat more calories than a chocolate recipe book. A very black cloud was starting to descend over me; I began to fall into a very dark place complete with even darker thoughts. I had never been in such a place before and was not sure whether the cause was me, the drugs, or some other entity!

I would cry myself to sleep at night, curled up in the foetal position, hoping that tomorrow would be better or that it had been a horrific nightmare.

For around four weeks, I closed myself off from everyone, including my family, which was one of the hardest things for them to witness. Here was their daughter who had been the life and soul of a party, a girl who had everything in life with much more to live for. What was really happening? Blood and urine tests were performed every couple of days. It became widespread practice for junior doctors and nurses alike to pay me visits to try and get an improved understanding of this illness. During one of these visits, a new consultant was introduced to me who advised me that he would be responsible for my ongoing kidney tests.

While lupus can have a multitude of side effects, some of the worst can involve damage to the vital organs. In previous cases noted, a small majority of lupus patients went on to suffer with kidney damage. After the consultant concluded all his relevant tests, he would return with his plan of care.

The news came as a bit of a shock even though knowing the kidneys had been affected, but treatment could slow down or stop the aggravation of the disease, so new medications were to be added to my already lengthy list. The structure of the treatment is something I was never quite aware of at that time. During the next few days, I was given cyclophosphamide and azathioprine together with steroids. Cyclophosphamide and azathioprine are part of the immunosuppressant drug family and have a damping effect during severe flare-ups of lupus. The cyclophosphamide was given intravenously during my last my few days in hospital, and the remaining five doses were administrated during the following six months.

CHAPTER 13

On returning home after my stay in hospital that year, I sat up, gathered my thoughts, and tried to pull myself together, but this was to prove too difficult. The weeks that followed were some of my darkest. I had turned into a person who had no control over her temper, could not hold a polite conversation with anybody, and started to hate the way I looked. A lot of my outbursts were taken out on family members, but on some occasions, they occurred in public. One has stayed with me for years. I had decided to take a drive to Carlisle, accompanied by both my father and grandfather. It was arranged that they would conduct the shopping while I waited for them in the car park. On entering the multi-storey car park, the cars started to queue round the levels. We continued up and soon located a space that soon would become available. As I sat with my indicator flashing and my foot on the accelerator, a car to my left decided to make a dash for the now available space. I do not really know what happened next, but I was soon out of the car and heading for the cheeky driver's car door. My father and grandfather were right on my heels. As I reached the door, I pulled the handle and was about to tell this man exactly what I thought when I was pulled back and marched back to the car. The sheer anger that day terrified me. It was not just the "red mist" thing; it was as if I had no control at all, and I am not sure what would have happened if my father had not been there. As the weeks continued, my medication was altered slightly, and the mood slowly started to lift.

Steroids can have all kinds of effects on your mind as well as your body. I became very self-conscious about my appearance and how the disease was starting to control me. The drugs were responsible for all my mood swings and temper outbursts and were turning me into a bit of a psycho to say the least. As with any drug, though, I followed medical advice and kept taking the pills daily. They had, in fact, reduced the inflammation. A decision I had to make overnight was, "Do I return to the pain and discomfort or deal with the mood swings?" I was left no option but to continue with the medication. One day while out shopping with my mother, we walked past a large shop window, and without warning I suddenly stopped in my tracks, looked back at the reflection in the window and saw not myself but a stranger who was looking back at me through my eyes. I just froze with shock, as it was the first time I had seen this image since beginning my treatment, tears ran down my swollen eyes and ballooned face. The way I looked, felt, and acted were affected by side effects of this illness and its treatment, and I did not like it one little bit.

During an appointment at the hospital, I was introduced to a social worker, who in turn helped me with everything from care costs to personal advice regarding my feelings. The help that I received at that time was much needed. There were many visits from both family and friends, but looking back, I see that talking to someone on neutral ground was a blessing. I started to gain more confidence in myself and soon was attending both my local doctor and clinic appointments. I would try and have a positive outlook during the following weeks, often thinking that things would have to turn soon, and I could get back to work.

CHAPTER 14

When I left school at sixteen, I had gone straight into work and had never been out of work for this length of time, not to mention that I had never claimed any monies from the state for sickness. When I was advised that I could applied for disability living allowance and other health costs, I completed the forms accordingly and waited. The forms were often long and drawn out, but all were answered truthfully, including that I had been driving myself to and from the local hospitals. During this time, the government was cracking down on people who were on certain allowances and really did not need them. When I received my mail the day the response came, I was not expecting to be classed as a benefit fraud. Well, that is what it made me feel like, as they had denied me the disability living allowance on the grounds that I drove myself to and from the hospital. It is interesting to note that with disability living allowance you can be selected for the mobility section as well as the carers section! I had mixed feelings with reference to the decision. My heart would tell me that I would be soon back to work, and this would make me more determined to do so, and then my head would tell me not to get angry and that what will be will be, and that's how it was left.

During the next three years, I stayed at home, recovering from medication and being totally bored. I would potter around the garden with Heather the German shepherd, my biggest fan; me; and my shadow, the loyal companion. Lupus eventually made me turn a huge corner during this time. I trawled books and magazines, trying to gain further knowledge on the illness. If anything, I wanted to help others through this wolf-in-sheep's-clothing illness. Initially at this time there were no local support groups, and I knew of nobody in the area who had suffered the extreme effects I had. During this time, the principal areas I wanted answers on were how and why one gets this illness. Some of the answers I found related to environment, heredity, and stress. I also found that lupus is more prevalent in African Caribbean women than any other race, with a low percentage of men being diagnosed.

CHAPTER 15

A t the beginning of 1996, I started to feel a lot stronger. I was still being prescribed many drugs and was rattled daily. At one point, I had more than twenty-seven tablets to take over a twelve-hour period. There were a few blips during that year, which included several DVTs (blood clots) in my legs, even though I was still taking warfarin! There were many drug options tried and evaluated on me during these times, some proved to be working and some like the warfarin proved otherwise. One large blip came during a weekend after my last DVT. I had been in hospital while they stabilized my blood clotting time and started me on another blood thinner called heparin. They advised me that if I wanted to return home for the weekend, I would have to manage to inject myself with the drug. Without hesitation, I was practising and soon got the hang of it, headed home, and started another recovery period. The Saturday night came, and I curled up on the sofa to watch a television programme while my parents went off to bed. While watching the television, I slowly made my way through a large bottle of lemonade, the only drink then that refreshed my mouth. As the hour went by, I noticed that I was becoming slightly short of breath. On sitting up, the pain seemed to increase, and soon I could not get away from the discomfort when breathing. My stomach ached and started to churn, and I began to feel sick. I had not had that much to eat during the day, but I wondered whether it could be food poisoning? I really was not sure.

I made it to the bathroom just in time as I started to vomit, and the diarrhoea was soon to follow. I really was not sure which would be the best option for me: *Do I jump on or off the loo, or do I just sit on the toilet with my head in the bath?* The latter turned out to be my only option, as I was there until the early hours of the morning. My mother sat with me in that bathroom, wiping and holding my head as I vomited. I eventually had no energy to even hold my head up. When we thought it had subsided for a while, she bundled me into the car, bucket and all, and headed for the infirmary. As it turned out, my mother could have been some sort of rally driver, and God help anyone or anything getting in her way! On our arrival, she located a wheelchair, and we made a dash for the lifts. As we approached the ward, the nurses came running; they had been informed of my return by my father back home. They assisted me straight into a room located right next door to the nurse's station.

The isolation room was quite like the room I had previously used when my migraines were present. Once inside, they undressed me and lay me on the bed. I had not been in that position for that long before the sickness started again. Where was it all coming from? Well, unbeknown to me, during that weekend, my kidneys were failing, and everything I was eating and drinking was poisoning me, so the only way my body could get rid of the substances was to vomit and excrete. In the next hour, I had a small tube inserted through my nose and down into my stomach to ease the sickness as well as to take the pressure off the stomach lining. A neckline was also fitted; it was located alongside the main jugular vein in my neck. This tube was around six inches long, with three smaller tubes that branched off the main one. They could not access any veins in normal areas like arms, hands, or even feet owing to the level of fluid I had accumulated on board, so they would use this neckline as the only other option available for the administration of medication. In total, I had put on an extra three stones of weight in fluid during that twenty-four-hour period. They injected me to ease both the sickness and the diarrhoea, and by lunchtime, the diarrhoea had stopped, but the sickness carried on up through the tube and continued into the attached bag.

Combined with being exhausted and feeling completely out of it, my eyes slowly closed, and I fell asleep. As my parents sat by my bedside, I thought back to twenty-four years previous, and the same worry and heartache overwhelmed me yet again. Within a couple of days, I started to sit up in bed and feel a bit more normal—though I loosely use the term "normal." Reducing the fluid that was on board was a slow process; I was to be injected with a diuretic, which would work alongside the kidneys to pass the excess water; during this process, I returned to about eleven stone in weight. The red marks that soon became apparent on my arms, legs, and stomach were stretch marks caused by the extreme fluid build-up over the previous days.

Following these days, the sickness subsided, and I started taking in both solid and liquid-based food. I do not know what my inside thought when I took my first mouthful; I felt slightly apprehensive, to say the least, as the stomach tube was still in place, but all was well, and soon the tube was to be removed. The following few days were a mixture of hesitation, and I was not sure what little surprises were round the next corner.

To anyone who has or is going through some sort of illness, the scale of the illness is irrelevant. Some of the best advice I can give anybody is to continue to listen to your body and never give up hope. This piece of advice, however, will often fall on deaf ears. Or, even worse, you may be told to go forth and so on! I remember hearing, when friends and family came to visit me in hospital, such things as "You will never see the wood for the trees" and "As the saying goes, time is the greatest healer." Believe me, I have heard them all, but I have to say that once you think it can't get any worse, it usually will; then and only then will you turn a corner. I can tell you till I am blue in the face how difficult the last few months were, but how I got through them I can only try and explain. At some point you will encounter people who will convince you that God and any other additional disciples out of the Bible will always take care of you. You may come across friends and family sending you blessings and poems from their personal beliefs, which may include such things as guardian angels. Whatever the gift, you will see the words as just words. Whatever the gifts you receive, they will have a very special meaning to you in either weeks, months, or even years to come; try not to dismiss them. In a moment you will look back, maybe while you're on your own road to recovery, and they will make you smile and remember.

There was an instance of this not long after I snapped at a friend of mine after being told "You're over the worst now" and "We can see the light at the end of the tunnel." It's not that you want to snap at loved ones; you can only progress in your way and in your own time. One of the most memorable gifts I was given during a low period was the poem "Footprints in the Sand"; on receiving it, I was not aware of the real meaning until a few days later.

CHAPTER 16

I had been in hospital now for around four weeks and was much improved from the day I was admitted but there was another test coming up—a kidney biopsy. A week before the biopsy was due, my blood was checked for clotting, and medication for this was stopped because I was classed as a high-risk patient owing to my previous DVT and pulmonary embolism—blood clot in the lung (PE). Next stop: the scan room! They led me into the treatment room where they would hunt for my kidneys and mark an entry point for the upcoming incision. But when someone says "biopsy," all sorts of wild ideas start swirling around in your mind. I mean, I could not help but flash back to my high school biology dissection class, imagining a monster needle plunging deep into my kidney and carving out a chunk! Okay, okay, laugh all you want, but it is true!

Let me tell you what really happens. After the scan, you lie on your front. The scanning apparatus is still present, and they use it again to confirm the location. A special hollow needle is then pushed through the skin and muscle and into the kidney tissue to obtain a small sample. Because of the local anaesthetic, you should not feel any pain. However, you may feel some pressure as the doctor pushes on the needle. The needle is inserted and withdrawn quickly, bringing with it a small sample of kidney tissue. You will be asked to hold your breath for five to ten seconds when the needle is pushed in and out (you will be told exactly when). This is because the kidneys move slightly when you breathe in and out. It is all over in about twenty minutes. The most surprising part for me was when I saw the needle. Yes, it's large, but the biopsy itself is the size of a spot of blood dripping from the needle. I was advised that with the information taken from this blood spot, they would be able to tell how much damage had been done to the kidneys—amazing!

Upon returning to the ward, I was instructed to lie on my back for several hours. The medical staff conducted routine tests, such as measuring my blood pressure and pulse, with meticulous attention to detail. I remained lying down until further notice, sitting up only later that night, and eventually getting out of bed.

At ten o'clock that night, two delightful nurses began their night shift as the previous shift ended. Not long after, I began to experience symptoms of indigestion. Initially the pain occurred only when I inhaled, but it rapidly intensified with each exhalation. Despite requesting peppermint juice from one of the nurses, the discomfort persisted even after its administration. During those fateful twenty minutes, I found myself closer than ever to facing my mortality. As I struggled to catch my breath while perched on the edge of the bed, I noticed an unusual pattern of nettle rash appearing on my legs. Suddenly a cool breeze touched my face, and I looked up to see my family standing behind the windows behind me. They cheered me on, but one person was notably absent: my grandmother Jean, who had passed away five years prior. At that moment, I heard her voice urging me not to give up but to keep fighting. Upon hearing her voice, it was as though a window had opened before me, and a gentle breeze caressed my face once more.

My next recollection is of me sitting upright in a different bed, connected to wires and leads that ran across my body. I had been transported to the intensive care unit, where they had successfully restored my heartbeat and revived me from wherever I had been before. This memory remains as vivid in my mind as if it had occurred yesterday. That night, two heroic angels in scrubs saved my life, although I could not grasp the full extent of it at the time. While respecting all beliefs and faiths, I could not help but wonder, *can miracles really happen?* The answer was a resounding yes, and I was hungry to learn more.

During this evening's trauma, these two nurses assisted me in bringing me back from the brink of death along with several other medical staff. There had been times when hope had faded and the worst was heading my way, but these nurses never gave up hope and prayed. Now, I would like to express here that I never fully understood the whole concept of the church, and I did not know then what I believed in, if anything. All I knew and felt was that something had happened that night, and these nurses had something to do with it. My parents were called during the night and told to attend the hospital as soon as they could and to be prepared for the worst.

When I came to the intensive care unit, I sat bolt upright in bed, trying to climb out. I started pulling at the wires, which in turn set the alarms off, which sent nurses running around everywhere. A completely different feeling ran through my veins after that disturbance—a feeling of energy and a new me. I thanked everybody the next day when I returned to my original room. I had suffered from a PE and had been extremely lucky to have come out of it alive.

During the next few days, I had my kidney tests done again, with some very strange results. One of the tests the doctors perform regarding kidney function is a creatinine test, which measures how well the kidneys are working. The day before I went for my kidney biopsy, the result was over 700 micromoles per litre, which is moderate to severe kidney failure. A couple of days after my attack, the blood result was shown at a level of 127 micromoles per litre, which was a significant drop from normal kidney function! How? I even had the medics baffled, and with no explanation given, I was only glad to be around to see it!

One more strange event was to be added to the happenings of that same night. More than twelve thousand miles away in Australia, my good old friend Christo in Sydney was attending a church meeting with friends when he asked the meeting to all pray for his friend who was in hospital, seriously ill. This event was related to me months later, and when the dates were checked, I realized it had been the same night in question! Was this a coincidence or the doing of a higher force? It is your choice. For me, knowing that my family was there on the other side, along with little angels handing out a little extra help, truly gave me extra strength. Personally, I think whatever entity you believe in or gives you support will offer you some of the best healing anyone can receive.

While I recovered days later, I often had lengthy conversations with the two nurses about what happened that night. Their replies may come as a bit of a shock to most, but their answers were basic. They replied that the power of prayer is all that is needed. I was still unsure about what my thoughts were regarding what really happened that night. One thing is for sure; without a doubt, both my grandmother and my guardian angel were with me during my adventure, and the words "fight on" certainly had meaning; the words stuck with me and always will.

There were many other people with whom I came into contact during my stay who would have an impact on my life, none more so than a certain physiotherapist. She was a very soft-spoken lady with whom I had many interesting conversations. One subject that struck a note with me was alternative therapies; she spoke about reiki, aromatherapy, acupuncture, reflexology, and many others. The medical world was still in a blinkered view regarding anything alternative, but the magazines and books I had been reading in the previous months were filled with all sorts of success stories.

I decided to try a reflexology treatment from the physiotherapist some days later and saw some amazing results. She would point out various toes and sections of my foot which represented areas on my body. As she already knew my medical history, she insisted that she would not ask any further questions and that she would allow the feet to do the talking. There were many more areas mentioned than I could remember, but as she had stated would happen, I was soon experiencing various feelings of either slight discomfort or numbness. When these feelings present themselves, it indicates a blockage regarding that system.

When someone tells you that he or she is going to massage your feet, various images and feelings run through your mind, such as "I have tickly or horrible feet," but these feelings were soon to be diminished as the heat from her hands covered the soles of my feet. As I lay, she sat at the bottom of my hospital bed and started to massage some oil into my very swollen, dry feet. The technique used was a firm but comfortable pressure covering the whole foot and the ankle joint. It was so relaxing that I nearly fell asleep, but at the same time, I became very intrigued about the whole concept. Every part of the body is mapped out in such a way that you can access all the systems through the feet. An example is the big toe, which is linked to the head and brain, eyes, and ears, and so on. Some areas that pressure was used in did, however, result in some level of discomfort; one such area turned out to be the kidneys. These treatments continued till I was soon allowed home. Unfortunately, due to the appointment times, my sessions had to end, but the experience never left my mind.

CHAPTER 17

O ver the next few weeks, I endeavoured to maintain a positive outlook, and eventually I was permitted to return home. The subsequent months were marked by a gradual recovery encompassing both physical and mental healing. During my hospitalization, the fluid buildup in my body had concealed my bones, making it feel as if I had hot water bottles tied to my legs. In fact, my feet had swollen so much that I had to buy slippers three sizes larger to accommodate them. However, after the fluid was drained, I could feel the bones around my ankle and observe the movement of my toes as I flexed the joints. I was finally able to recognize my feet, ankles, and legs again.

During the later part of 1996, I was gaining both strength and determination to return to work. There were all kinds of ideas running around my head regarding what I should do and whether I should return to the travel agent or try something new? In a way, I knew I had been given a fresh start of some sort. I was at a bit of a loose end when, unexpectedly, I received a call from some long-lost friends in London. "Come down and stay for a weekend and see how you feel" were the words used. Well, what did I have to lose? I arranged to stay with my friends with what turned out to be more than a weekend. Instead, it was a few weeks. I managed to locate a job as a travel agent, and this is what I did for a couple of months before I moved into my own rented accommodation. Together with new friends and work colleagues, I was soon leading a normal life with happy memories of meeting friends for coffee or heading into the city for dinner. As new circles were being created, new opportunities were also raising their heads. Soon I started to move around and work in the areas of travel and telesales, and then I finally made my last move into marketing. The computer telesales position was quite a move for me, as I knew nothing about computers; I could not even tell the difference between a hard drive and a port hole! It is funny looking back now. If you really want something that much, you can turn your hand to anything, especially when you need the money. The computer business was about to take off, and the timing was perfect. As modern technology developed, we were soon discovering newer and smaller mobile phones, together with faster computers than we had previously used. It was quite an exciting time, especially for a person who lived for her mobile phone!

Towards the end of 1998, I decided I was always a country girl underneath and craved the countryside. Once the decision was made, I returned to my parents' home in the borders. The idea of settling down and being content with the status quo never even crossed my mind. Whatever I was doing was but a stepping stone to something bigger and brighter. My destination? Well, that was anyone's guess, except for one thing I was sure about, and that was that I still had to combat my desire to travel the world. I still believe to this day in the saying "What is for you will not pass you by," and looking back during my working life, things always seemed to slot into place—maybe not at the desired time, but for the correct reasons. So, picture this: I am chilling at home when suddenly a wild travel agent appears! But here is the twist: this time around, the agent offered me the ultimate dream job in the travel industry, which I loved so much. Talk about fate, right? In this job, I got to jet-set to some of the most incredible places on the planet: Dubai, East Asia, and even good ol' America.

But wait, there is more! I also made a triumphant return to Australia, though the first trip down under was quite a surprise, to say the least. The Australian Tourist Board had recently organized a competition that offered an exciting prize package of two weeks on the Great Barrier Reef, along with a weeklong PADI diving course. As a keen participant in their training programme over the previous months, I diligently completed the requisite exercises in preparation for my final exams, which led to my being awarded the coveted Australian specialist title. This title granted me access to discounted fares and accommodation across Australia. The competition required a personal sentence answer, with no restrictions on the nature of the response.

As the weeks passed and the closing date came, I decided to visit one of my favourite clairvoyants. The conversation flowed about past and present details, and then the lady in question stated that a visit overseas would be coming up, but not as I expected. I left that day convinced that I would be heading off to Australia very soon. A few days passed after the closing date, and still I had not heard anything. I decided to call up the competition line and inquire about the winners. Once the call was picked up, I relayed my question to the operator. "One moment, please; I will transfer you. Hold the line," bellowed down the line. One thing I cannot stand is being passed from pillar to post, firing out the same questions and getting nowhere fast, or being told I will have to call back. Eventually I got through to another lady who gave me the devastating news that they had picked all the winners for the competition, and that was that. The conversation was soon picked up again by the lady, and for some reason, I jokingly said that I would help with the cases, or any other help needed for that matter! We laughed and joked before she advised that the only thing she could think that might help, but with no guarantee, was that the winners had to perform a dive in their local swimming pool before accepting their win. If any winners went along to their swimming pool to dive and then discovered it was not for them, they would decline the offer, thus wasting time overseas. Either way, I left my telephone number, and I waited and waited, fingers crossed and phone in hand, waiting for a glimmer of hope. Meanwhile, I turned to a trusty friend for help, who took me on an underwater adventure at the local pool. Suddenly I was hooked—or was this all a big waste of time?

Just a day later, my phone rang and a lovely lady from the tourist board confirmed that one of the lucky winners had turned down the diving trip. Then, faster than a dolphin can swim, she asked, "Do you want to go?" Without hesitation, I shouted, *Yes, please!* Hold on to your seats, folks! This was not just any trip.

In just a few weeks, we were off to the land down under, with a squad of ten adventure-loving explorers. We are all gaga for Australia, but for me this was a return to my happy place. The journey kicked off with a flight from London, with a cheeky pit stop in Singapore before we hit the destination: Brisbane! But wait, there is more! We then boarded a tiny seaplane that took us to the jewel of the crown—Heron Island on the Great Barrier Reef! Get ready to be blown away!

I ventured to the Gold Coast with no idea what to expect, but boy, was I in for a treat! Nestled on a coral cay, Heron Island is the *only* swanky resort smack in the middle of the Great Barrier Reef. It is like a dream come true: imagine dipping your toes into the crystal-clear water and wading into a wonderland of coral reefs bursting with colourful marine life. It is like a real-life mermaid adventure!

We kicked off our exotic journey at Brisbane International Airport, where we grabbed our bags and headed straight for Gladstone Airport. The cherry on top of our adventure? A small seaplane that would take us to Heron Island! As soon as we landed, we were mesmerized by the view from our lodges. Our jaws dropped at the sight of the blue sea stretching out before us. And once we stepped inside, we were greeted by cosy twin beds, a TV, and a patio that opened straight onto the golden sands of the beach. The sound of the waves crashing against the shore was within arm's reach!

One early morning, I was startled by an unfamiliar scratching sound emanating from the patio doors. My curiosity piqued, I approached the door, only to discover a loggerhead turtle clawing at the sand. Given the strict guidelines governing the observation of nesting and hatching turtles, I discreetly took a photo before retreating behind the curtains to witness the scene. Heron Island is renowned globally for its awe-inspiring coral reef, a diverse range of aquatic life, migrating whales, nesting turtles, and abundant birdlife. Additionally, it offers some of the best diving opportunities worldwide. After feasting on a scrumptious breakfast, we donned our diving gear and headed for the pool, ready to take on new underwater adventures.

For the next five days, we dove deep and learned all about deflating, inflating, and sharing masks underwater, while discovering depths we never knew existed! Everything was a thrill until the fateful day when we set sail for the vast blue ocean. We were a bundle of nerves yet were bursting with excitement. Common sense would tell you that jumping off a boat with a weight around your waist is a recipe for disaster, but we were ready to take the plunge! Hey, do not take this the wrong way, but we seemed like mermaid statues bobbing around, all silent and stoic. This was because of the excitement ahead and the overwhelming scene below! Our trek to the reef's edge was mind-blowing, but not in a scary way. Instead, the fish, the hues, and the stingrays and sharks had me gobsmacked and gasping for air! Picture this: we are diving deep, and suddenly we are given exercises to perform. But wait, these are not like the ones we practised in the pool! Amid all this underwater action, I am suddenly surrounded by sea creatures, some of them getting a little too close for comfort. It is as if I am in a whole new world, feeling overwhelmed and free all at once. Seriously, it is a journey worth taking. I dare you to dive in and explore the breathtaking scenery—no glass tanks allowed!

During the last week of our adventure, we headed for Brisbane, a city bursting with arts and culture, to spend relaxing hours wandering around the shops and boutiques. During our trip, I conversed with our tour guide about our shared interest in health and complementary therapies. The guide shared her inspiring journey of overcoming ovarian cancer and expressed confidence in my ability to overcome my past health issues. We discussed various treatments, but what caught my attention was her explanation of how a person's blood type determines his or her dietary requirements. I was intrigued by this concept and intended to further research this and explore detailed readings on this topic upon my return home.

It was a grand finale to one of the wildest, most thrilling adventures of my life. My satisfaction levels were through the roof! During my tenure as a travel agent, I had the opportunity to participate in several trips sponsored by various tourist boards. These trips proved to be invaluable in expanding my knowledge of different resorts and hotels, enhancing my understanding of the expectations of the travelling public. With each subsequent trip, my awareness of the needs and preferences of travellers grew, providing me with a greater insight into the industry.

aged 2

Mewith bobby

Me & Bobby

Mum and I

Grandma & Grandad Wright

dad with Steven & I

First glassses

Me on the rocking horse

The big house

The Riding

Me and hobo 1st pony

Last day at the red lion

Steven & Tara's wedding

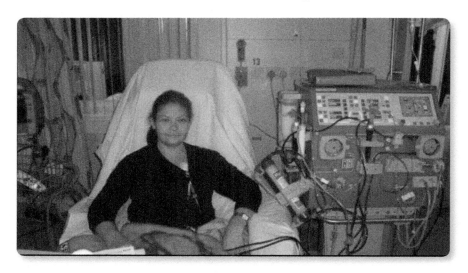

2010 dec diayzsing

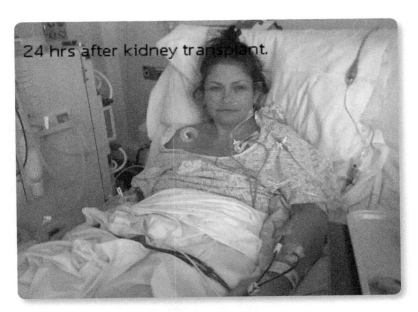

Kidney transplant

HGV Days

Betty common riding 2014

Harry showing

The team Travis, Betty & Harry

Diane's Reflexology

CHAPTER 18

As I reflect on my knowledge of Kielder, I wonder about the availability of provisions for disabled travellers at hotels and airports. Furthermore, travel requirements have undergone a shift, with many opting for personalized arrangements, including selecting flights and durations of stay in multiple destinations. The emergence of budget-friendly flights and customizable travel options has redefined the travel industry, leading to the decline of traditional high-street travel agents. This marks the onset of cost-effective travel arrangements powered by the Internet.

While living in London and upon my return to the borders, my health issues never surfaced. However, I was always apprehensive about their recurrence. During my visit to Australia, I engaged in a discussion with a tour guide who recommended a booked call *The Eat Right Diet* by Dr Peter D'Adamo. Intrigued, I acquired the book to gain further insight. The book revealed some striking characteristics, such as the origins of blood types and the correlation between certain foods and various health problems ranging from allergies to sickness. As an individual with a B+ blood type, I recently discovered that certain foods, such as chicken, tomatoes, and wheat are not recommended for my blood type. This revelation led me to ponder whether I had been inadvertently harming my body for years, even since birth. The idea seemed plausible, especially after learning about the origins of blood types. In my case, my blood type is associated with Africa, South America, and some Northern European regions. Somewhere in my lineage, there is a connection to Africa. My grandmother, Ethel, although not African, did possess a darker complexion, and I learned that lupus is more prevalent in African and Caribbean populations. My diet primarily consisted of chicken salads with tomatoes and bread as a filler. I made a deliberate choice to discontinue all medication and adhere strictly to the diet. My goal was to demonstrate my resilience and maintain good health without relying on prescription drugs and the associated side effects that I struggled with daily. I initiated my diet regimen in the early 2000s, and it has been my lifestyle ever since.

Upon relocating back to the north, I resumed consultations with my kidney specialist at the local hospital. These appointments were primarily to ensure my lupus remained under control and as a precautionary measure. During these consultations, my consultant would inquire about my medication and general health. In one such appointment, I was asked to state the medication I was taking, causing sheer panic to run through me, and I hesitated to answer. Had I disrupted my physical well-being by discontinuing my medication and seeking alternative medical treatments? During my consultation with the doctor, he leaned back, flashing a smile, and remarked that my latest blood tests were the best he had seen in years, even prior to my illness. Overjoyed by this news, I admitted that I had ceased taking all medication and was adhering to a blood diet. His sceptical look screamed volumes, but he gave me permission to keep on keeping on. And boy, am I glad I did! Suddenly my mood and weight took a U-turn, and I felt alive in a way I had not in ages. I had more pep in my step felt I was facing a brighter tomorrow. It was like banishing an annoying shadow that had been haunting me. I was ready for a fresh start, and nothing could stop me!

One moment, I was sitting at the travel agency desk, and the next, I knew I had to follow my heart and explore the world. Do not get me wrong; travel agents are great, but it was not the highest-paying gig around. I needed something that would let me live my dream and rake in the dough. While catching up with my brother, who was a lorry driver for a local company, I asked him about his day-to-day life on the open road. I even prodded him for any potential bumps in the road if I were to follow in his tyre tracks. After some deep chats, I concluded that I was all in for some heavy-duty training! It was the end of the year 2000, and I was about to embark on a secret mission. I enrolled in heavy goods training, but guess what? I did not tell a soul, not even my family! Back then you could spot only a handful of lady truckers on the road, so it was quite an unusual career choice for a woman. Learning to drive a truck was a wild ride, to say the least. Here I was, standing at five feet four inches and grappling with a steering wheel that looked about the same size as me! The transmission had more gears than a Boeing 747, and the forty-five-foot trailer tagged along like a lost puppy. The training was like driving a car but multiplied by a gazillion! It was mirror, signal, and manoeuvre, but on a larger-than-life scale.

Driving a lorry has its advantages, one of which is the elevated position that offers an enhanced view of the surroundings as compared to a car. However, becoming proficient behind the wheel of such a vehicle requires mastery of its length and width, along with an understanding of its unique characteristics with respect to other road users. Proper coaching is essential to ensure adherence to legal road speeds, navigating roundabouts with care, and maintaining awareness of other vehicles. Unlike car driving lessons, where instructors can take control of the vehicle, in the case of a lorry, the driver is solely responsible for operating the vehicle. So, I thought it would be a promising idea to try reversing, but boy was I wrong! I just could not wrap my head around turning the wheel in the opposite direction. The result? I ended up either crushing the cones or jack-knifing the trailer.

When you are cruising on the UK's motorways in a heavy goods vehicle, you are not exactly setting any land speed records. Thanks to a speed limiter, the max speed is 60 mph. And once you hit minor and single carriageways, you will be crawling at 40 mph. As a newbie, I had to navigate through a crazy number of gears—up to sixteen in total! But once you hit that sweet spot, there is no stopping you! Now, you might be thinking, "What's with all these gears?" But trust me, they are crucial. Skipping a gear in a lorry is like missing a beat in a dance routine; it can throw off your entire flow. During my first driving test, the examiner kept a keen eye on me, making sure I was shifting gears seamlessly for take-off and such. But with the pressure on, my mind wandering to the upcoming reversing test, I accidentally skipped not one, but two gears! The lorry bounced like a bunny before coming to a jolting stop. The instructor frantically reached for the dashboard as the vehicle swerved but was yanked back by her seatbelt. It was as clear as day—my journey for a heavy goods licence had hit a roadblock, and another test was in order. Two attempts later, I finally hit the jackpot and cruised to success. Once again, this was a test that proved its worth. It was a thrilling new adventure to be behind the wheel of a heavy goods vehicle. After passing, I was uncertain what job opportunities would be available, considering most required at least two years of prior experience. It seemed paradoxical, and it left me wondering how one could gain experience without starting somewhere. However, I managed to secure a position working the night shift at a nearby distribution centre, where I remained for a year, acquiring valuable driving and work experience.

CHAPTER 19

In early 2001, the countryside along the borders endured a severe farming crisis as foot-and-mouth disease spread rapidly. The affected areas were marked by plumes of black smoke rising from fields, resembling a massive bonfire. Within days of the disease's confirmation, farmers resorted to lighting their burning fires.

The Burning of Livestock: A Personal Account

In the past, farmers would burn their own livestock, and often the burning would take place near or within sight of the main farmhouses. I can still vividly recall those days, along with the unmistakable stench that permeated everything. It clung to your hair and clothes and even seeped into your skin. I had heard that they were looking for heavy goods drivers to help transport dead livestock, and initially I thought it might be an interesting new experience with a tipping trailer. It had never occurred to me just how many dead animals I would encounter in this line of work. Just down the road, the action was booming, and I could not resist following the buzz!

Back in the early days, the army was called in to wrangle the endless line of lorries, waiting to head off to the next farm. But then, from out of nowhere, a fiery-haired young chap with a thick Glaswegian accent and a sexist swagger popped up and caught me off guard! Now I realized that I was in the lion's den, surrounded by the meanies who could make or break me with a snap of their fingers. But "break" was not even a word in my vocabulary as I stood there, remembering my wise grandpa's words. During an interview, I was asked if I had experience driving a tipper and when I could commence work. I pondered briefly and replied that I had driven a forty-five-foot boxed trailer before, which should not differ much from driving a tipping trailer. I confirmed that I could begin working the following day. Praise the authorities, someone was watching over me that day! I was being nervous, hoping I would not be assessed on my knowledge of tipping trailers—because I was clueless!

The next day, I saw that same red-haired chap, but he did not make a peep as I strode to the head office. They tossed me some protective gear and truck keys, and I made a beeline back to the tipping trailers. I figured that if I could suss out my surroundings before heading to the farm, I would not be the typical "ditsy girl" in what was clearly a male-dominated environment. As I swaggered up to my trusty lorry, a couple of seasoned drivers popped up from out of nowhere. Over the months, I had heard all sorts of jabs and wisecracks—some cheeky, some downright sassy. But, hey, you just got to take it all on the chin and let out a good laugh, right? It is all part of the driving adventure! Picture this: a group of experienced drivers, wiser than Yoda himself, became my guardian angels during the foot-and-mouth outbreak. They schooled me on all things regarding tipping trailers, gave me the lowdown on grumpy nonbelievers of female drivers, and even shared their secret breakfast spots! These fine folks became my lifelong friends, and together we faced the foot-and-mouth disaster with ease.

After the burning fires were stopped, the new pits were opened deep inside local forests and landfills. The pits had been dug out, and every load was to be disposed of in them and then covered over again. During the first three months, I was located up in the Scottish borders, where every single farm was cleared out. Sheep and cattle all were slaughtered; during the springtime, even newborn lambs fell victim. In the weeks that followed, I witnessed heart-wrenching scenes as farmers, their families, and workers saw their entire livelihoods disappear before their eyes. It was a distressing time, and I came to realize that my driving career was male dominated. Despite feeling the same sense of upset as those around me, I knew that it was essential to remain composed and not reveal my emotions.

Amidst the summer heat, the dreaded foot-and-mouth disease raged on, prompting my relocation from the Scottish Borders to Yorkshire. I was met with a new challenge—smaller farms with longer routes, making it hard to haul cargo. Thankfully, eight-wheeler tippers came to the rescue! After sitting around for weeks, I finally took on the challenge of driving these beasts, marking the start of yet another exciting chapter of learning! The foot-and-mouth outbreak led to the continued disposal of animals, causing significant concern among farms and farmers. This period was marked by immense hardship and personal loss that would continue to impact British farming for years to come.

After the foot-and-mouth fiasco, I hustled on with my eight-wheeled friend, rolling through towns and cities. I landed a gig in the charming Bedfordshire, where I spent a solid two years learning the ropes. But, like all restless souls, I started feeling a bit anxious. Nevertheless, my time in Bedfordshire was a treasure trove of experience and wisdom, and that is what it is all about! I had always been interested in driving a lorry on the continent. However, the prospect of driving on the opposite side of the road was a concern for me. Nevertheless, I kept reassuring myself that I could adapt to the change if I tried. While reading a trucking magazine, I stumbled upon a new fascination that piqued my interest. A new contract had been given to a company in Nottingham, travelling back and forth to Gibraltar. *Perfect!* I thought. I could do this. And I did! I spent the next twelve months travelling back and forth to Gibraltar, covering France, Spain, and Portugal, with some encounter's stranger than others.

On my first day, an experienced driver made a beeline towards me, clutching a small plastic bag. The conversation was short yet sweet, and unexpectedly, he handed me the bag, saying, "This might come in handy someday." Curiously, inside was a pair of miniature straps, one with a solid metal frame halfway down, perfect for tightening against objects. These sturdy straps are usually seen on large low loaders, holding down hefty farm machinery. I extended my gratitude and got cracking, making sure my lorry was all set for its journey.

The first few trips were downright nerve-racking, and if I am honest, I do not recall too much of it. But hey, I got to the destination and back in one piece, so no harm done. The drill was simple: collect groceries and frozen goods and transport them straight to a sweet supermarket in Gibraltar. Easy-peasy! The return journey became my favourite aspect of the trip, since it was always a delightful surprise to visit diverse locations, cities, and even countries to collect produce for transportation to the UK. Typically, our haul consisted of an array of vegetables, including various kinds of potatoes, tomatoes, and peppers. On rare occasions, we even transported wine. The journey back home was like a treasure hunt, with each trip bringing fresh excitement and discoveries! I could not wait to see where we would end up, hopping from one city to another, and sometimes even crossing borders to gather the most scrumptious veggies. Our loot was like a rainbow of colours, including spuds, tomatoes, and peppers of all kinds, as well as the occasional bottle of wine! As a professional driver, one becomes well-versed in the driving regulations in both the UK and the continent. These regulations are in place to ensure the safety and well-being of all drivers. To comply with the law, there are specific maximum driving hours and mandatory rest periods within a twenty-four-hour cycle. So, picture me zipping around Bordeaux, totally lost, and running out of time. In a split second, I made a move that could have gone terribly wrong. At a red light, I hopped out of my cab and dashed over to the driver in front of me. And guess what? A guy's face stared back at me! But wait, there is more! He spoke English! Who knew?

"Excuse me, kind sir, can you help me locate this address?" I asked, hoping for a positive response. Instead, he finished my sentence and motioned for me to follow him. With the traffic light turning green, I climbed back into the cab, and we zoomed off. Talk about a risky adventure! Who knew where he could have taken me?

It was a moonless night, and the only sound was the distant hum of lorries in the industrial estate. My nerves were feeling a bit jittery as we took turns one after another. Suddenly we arrived at a pair of towering eight-foot iron gates. I clutched the door handle and locked myself in, wondering where we had ended up. My companion hopped out and strode towards the lorry door. I cracked the window open and bellowed, "This is the place!"

With a grin, the man made his way back to his car, leaving me slightly shaky inside. Suddenly the world around me began to shift, as in those suspenseful movies where the music builds, and you know something is about to jump out at you. I spotted a tiny glimmer of light coming from what seemed like a little cabin about a hundred metres from where I was standing. There was no sign of the company name and no entry sign for deliveries or pickups—just a mysterious light in the distance, beckoning me to explore.

As I geared up for my mission, I grabbed the lorry phone and jotted down the address, ready for my daring adventure. Like a secret agent, I approached the ominous gates, scanning for a way in. At most places, you would expect an intercom or some kind of access system, but these gates were something else! Gigantic and imposing, they loomed over me. Suddenly I noticed a tiny gate clicking open on the side. It was like a secret passage! There he was—a tiny man with jeans that had seen better days and a polo shirt. His hair was going grey and looked as if it had had a fight with a comb and lost. As he mumbled away in French, his face twisted as if I were crashing his party. I kept grinning, hoping my northern charm would work its magic and turn his frown upside down!

This was going to be challenging work. Still smiling, I asked if I was in the right place from the small handwritten address I had. "Wee" he replied. *Oh, thank the lord for that*, I thought as I wiped the beads of sweat off my brow. He slammed the towering gates shut and began a lengthy lecture about how I had to move my truck to a car park and then unlock the rear doors. This is standard protocol when your trailer is empty. Curtain-sided trailers are more susceptible to theft, given the ease of accessing their contents. To counter this, drivers often open either partially or open curtains. However, in the case of fridge trailers, having only barn doors at the back, opening one or both doors may indicate to potential thieves that the trailer is empty. As the small man started to walk away, he waved his hand at a small sign nearby that showed the company name, and along it was an image of a wine bottle and glass. Okay, so I was collecting wine! This made complete sense now. My little friend at the gate had been fully emerged in a good film with an extra-large glass of wine! We both parted company, with me heading to the rear of the trailer and him back to his film. He mumbled some words and threw his hand to the side of his head like someone shooting a gun at his head. It did not take long for the action of the gun to convey to me that this place was notorious for alcohol theft. My feet went into overdrive as I dashed towards the open back doors. I clambered onto the cab's steps, switched on the ignition, and waited for the seat to inflate and adjust. With a few deep breaths, I tried to calm myself and collect my thoughts. Suddenly it hit me that I had to shut the windows and sunroof. It did not take long for me to recall the plastic bag with my trusty straps in it. I strapped the living daylights out of both doors and gave them a firm tug. Mission accomplished! That night I dozed with one eye open and one closed. The rising of the sun stirred me in the early morning, and without a second thought I was up and in the driver's seat. I had not even got undressed. Heading for the door, I saw that there were a few more people about, and one man caught my eye.

As I pulled up in my lorry, he caught a glimpse of me and started flailing his arms, signalling he would open the gate. We have all been there; unfamiliar places can make us look like clowns, and being a female driver does not make it any easier! I had to put my big girl pants on! Listen, I will let you in on a secret: I despise being watched, especially when I am behind the wheel. It is as if every single person is waiting for me to mess up, and heaven forbid I oversteer or make one tiny mistake—everyone will be sure to notice!

I hopped onto a British-based lorry, which meant it was left-handed. Every spot I had been to in Europe was designed for right-handed lorry parking bays, which take some serious motor skills to nail. It is like driving in the dark with your eyes closed! When I was learning how to manoeuvre the mammoth lorry, I had to master the art of parking. I had to get used to the length and know what was around the vehicle. Sure, you can spot all corners of the truck, but it is like backing up your car or caravan with one eye closed. That blind spot is a doozy! Navigating the continent was never easy, especially when I was a lone ranger with a tricky task ahead. *Help!* I thought. But as I pulled up to the winery's bays, I found I was in luck! There was plenty of room to manoeuvre, and a crowd of onlookers—twenty men and a female cleaner—all were watching me! No pressure, right? With a deep breath, I backed up the fridge and beeped my way into the bay. *Phew.* Just one nudge, and voila!

The angels were shining down on me that day. Oh, the tales I could spill for days in this book. But let us save those gems for another time!

One memory that will stick with me forever is when I stopped at a Spanish fuel station, a man approached me and offered to pay me £15,000 for each immigrant that I would take back to the UK. He pointed to a minibus full of immigrants. I refused to have anything to do with it knowing it was illegal. When I arrived at the next toll station, I was approached by police officers with sniffer dogs, and they searched my lorry. Of course, were no immigrants just a lorry full of potatoes! Looking back, I sometimes wonder how I pulled off these wild adventures. Is it a superpower that comes with age? Regardless, one thing is for sure: every experience, good or bad, taught me a valuable lesson and added some serious bragging rights to my memory bank. So let those crazy moments fortify your backbone and make memories that will last a lifetime. I had my HGV wings now, hauling my HGV across the continent, covering Spain and France for a sweet twelve months. But, alas, my company lost the contract, and I was left wondering what to do next. I headed back to the borders and stayed with my folks while I plotted my next move. I was not going to let myself become a lost cause, so I hotfooted it to the agency drivers and got cracking on some jobs. One day it was milk tankers, the next it was tippers, but the true love of my trucking life was the fridge work. I felt like a genius, juggling loads of goods while being a champion at setting the perfect fridge temperatures.

CHAPTER 20

Unexpectedly, I felt a zing of inspiration: reflexology was calling my name! I had squirrelled away some cash, and the time had come to make my dream a reality. I have no idea where this sudden urge came from, but I was ready to take the plunge! I needed a job that was doable and did not break the bank while I was still on the payroll. So, I hit the web to find some courses that would give me a legit qualification, not just a crash course in the basics. Life lesson alert! Whenever you feel as if you are hitting a wall, just pause. Trust me; in hindsight, you will see why there were so many roadblocks. This was exactly what happened when I was hunting for the Scotland School in Falkirk. Every time I landed on their website; it was as though I hit a digital freeze. But hey, the universe had bigger plans for me! I have seen some real doozies online, with ads for health supplements or bogus companies with fake phone numbers. But, to my relief, I chatted with the school principal, who cleared up all my concerns. Picture it: a two-year, part-time course in the heart of Falkirk, Scotland. I was determined to have my cake and eat it too so I could study *and* earn some cash. The course was no joke; it covered everything from reflexology to anatomy and physiology. It was like a brain boot camp!

The cherry on top of the whole programme was the ten case studies that gave me a chance to get hands-on and dive deeper into the world of reflexology. It was a thrilling experience to see how the human body responds to the art of reflexology techniques, and my favourite part by far. The clients I reached out to years ago are still dear friends or delighted customers to this day! I asked all my clients if I could treat them to six weekly sessions, totally on the house and in the comfort of their own homes. Some had heard of reflexology, but others were excited to try something new. It was like peeking through a window into their physical and emotional worlds. As I worked my magic, I learned about their minds, bodies, and souls, and it was a never-ending source of enlightenment. Back in the day, I had a front-row seat to some incredible transformations. As I scribbled notes during our weekly six-week session, I could not help but notice the jaw-dropping changes happening to people's bodies. In the areas of hormones, aches and pains, and mental wellness, it was like watching superheroes emerge from their cocoons! Some treatments can stir up a storm of emotions, and boy, can they be life-changing! Folks would leave the session feeling different, and boy, oh boy, would they sleep like babies! I loved checking in on them the next day to hear all about their experience. It is still my favourite part of the treatment! Oh, the good old days!

The year 2004 was when I made the cut and our school invited locals to come and join our classroom sessions to help us hone our practical skills. In the mornings, we tackled the bookish parts of anatomy and philosophy. And let me tell you, it was a real revelation! At first it was cool not knowing anything about the clients and their issues, but then, as we dived deeper into their feet, we started to uncover all sorts of juicy titbits they had not shared before. I would whip out my trusty notepad and take detailed notes on every health issue my client shared. It was like collecting puzzle pieces, with each piece being a vital part of the reflexology experience. We all know when our tummy grumbles or our emotions run wild, but the whys and hows are just as important. It is all about connecting the dots, and I was eager to piece together a complete picture.

Life is a tangled web of connections all beginning with one vital system: your nervous system. And boy, oh boy, let me tell you, when one system hits a snag, it can send shockwaves through your whole body. It is like peeling an onion, layer by layer, and exposing all kinds of unusual twists and turns. Sure, it can be a bit painful for some people, but once you get to the core, the real healing begins. Just keep in mind that the healing process can sometimes get a little bumpy before it smooths out, but that is all part of the journey! I say "some people" above, as some people have what I would call a brick wall protecting them—or more to the point, hindering them. These layers can be years old or even forwarded from parents or guardians. I learned more about this a few years later. After I qualified in 2004, I carried on with the clients I used in my apprenticeship time. I would travel to people's homes and offer a mobile service. The clients which I had spent time with were continuing their own journeys as well as telling their friends and family. I think everyone from a background of working and making a wage, when thinking of transitioning to a new direction, feels the struggle both mentally and emotionally. Picture it: It was 2004, and I was newly qualified and eager to start my journey as a reflexologist. I decided to stick with my roots and keep serving the clients I worked with during my apprenticeship days. So, I lugged my gear all over town, bringing the experience to my clients' homes. This paid off big time! My loyal clients kept coming back and spreading the word to their own people. Let us be real, whether you are shifting careers or not, the mental and emotional struggle is real. But with a little grit and determination, anything is possible!

Leaping from a steady paycheque to the unknown world of entrepreneurship is a roller coaster of emotions. My advice? Take it step by step and stay positive! That is how I did it. On days off, I would gather a few curious minds and their friends to join us. Looking back, I realize I was still learning with every meeting. Who needs baby steps when you can sprint? That has always been my motto, and during this time, my inner curious cat was in overdrive. So, I fired a few questions at my clients, wondering what they thought about my consultation form. Specifically, I asked them how they would feel if I did not ask any questions at all. After much training with my clients, I decided to put my skills to the test on their friends, family, and random folks I had never met before. I was not trying to show off or anything; I just wanted to see if my hard work was paying off. I mean, can feet really reveal our deepest secrets? The results were mind-blowing! I still used the old tricks I learned in school, but the consultation part was out the window. It was like playing footsie with fate! Something magical was happening during my treatments. My hands were dialled up to a new frequency, noticing the slightest vibrations and temperature changes in my client's feet. They even started reporting wild new sensations they had never felt before! It was as if we were all discovering a brand-new universe together. I let my clients lead the way, telling me when they were ready for the next session. And do you know what? That is still how I roll with my clients today!

After months of honing my practice, fascinating new revelations were coming my way! It is tricky to articulate the feelings that arise from a mysterious energy exchange between two people. But there was one client I will never forget. We did not have that energy connection before, but something special was brewing as we got to work. We did not discuss any annoying ailments, new or old. The feet were our gateway to the soul, and boy, did we explore! Mix-and-match finger sensations, and even getting a grip on specific foot areas, were all part of the game. But taking a deep breath and holding a spot near the solar plexus while working on a client's feet was a meaningful change. A wave of tingly excitement washed not just over my fingers but all the way down to my toes as well! But when I asked the client if there were any sensations no sensations, no feelings, no nothing! Wild, right?

This experience hit me like a ton of bricks, so I whipped out my notepad and started scribbling. I could not help but wonder whether certain reflexes were more intense for people with specific ailments or whether I was just imagining things. Not only were my emotions all over the place, but I also noticed new sensations in my feet. The reflexes had different textures and patterns, and it was as though a whole new world had opened!

Whenever I worked on a sensitive area like a sore throat or a crunchy chest, my throat would start to tickle, and I would get the urge to cough! Was my body trying to process what was happening? It was like a mini-inner struggle! Feeling lost, I turned to fellow therapists for guidance, and they all pointed me towards reiki. I had heard whispers of this mystical practice, but the Internet was a baby back then, so I hit up the library for answers. But, alas, the books I read left me feeling as if I were chasing a white rabbit; none of them could explain my emotions. Picture Carlisle, a charming border city in Cumbria, England. There I was, juggling my little business *and* working as an HGV driver. Crazy, right? But it was worth it, because my business was booming! And let me tell you, after a long shift, I could not wait to get my hands (and feet) on my reflexology clients!

One regular weekend, a mysterious flyer slid through my door, offering sample massages and reiki. Fate works in funny ways, doesn't it? I had no idea these local therapists even existed, yet here they were, calling out to me with their magical healing powers. I stumbled upon this little oasis of a hall and spotted a lady by a cosy therapy couch that was decorated with the prettiest cushions and blankets. After a brief introduction, she offered me a tasty little fifteen-minute sample of reiki therapy. I was intrigued, having never had a taster before, so I jumped at the chance! My shoes were stashed under the couch, and as I lounged there, fully dressed, she draped a cosy throw over me. I had no clue what to expect, but a choice of heat, tingly sensations, or even colours flooded my body. With my eyes shut, I surrendered to the mystery. I cannot recall much from the session except for warm, fuzzy waves that rippled through my head. It was enchanting, and I was eager for more! After leaving that afternoon, I snagged the lady's card and offered a reflexology exchange. The firsthand education and insights gained were worth more than gold! If you are looking to up your wellness game or start a new career path, I highly recommend taking the time to train and qualify in reiki. Working with a reiki master gave me a new perspective on how to navigate the energies I was feeling and how to protect myself. It was a real revelation to realize that, yes, I was noticing people's vibes.

CHAPTER 21

As we zoomed towards 2007, I was racking up some serious experience, and my client roster was on the up and up. Suddenly the perfect chance to run a shop in Northumberland appeared before me, and I could finally kick driving to the curb! Listen up, risk-takers! If you are itching to take the leap into entrepreneurship, pause for a second and think it through. Going from a dependable paycheque to being your own boss is important. But when I fused beauty treatments with holistic health, I hit the jackpot. Not only did it attract beauty buffs, but it also brought together a community of wellness fans who were keen to experience the healing touch of holistic therapy. With a team of talented beauticians, we created a haven where people could enjoy the best of both worlds! I was a multitasking wizard, dividing my time between the shop and my on-the-go customers. I was like a superhero, zooming across Dumfries and Galloway, Cumbria, and Northumberland to keep up with my loyal clientele. And boy, did they keep coming from all corners, stamping in with innovative ideas and projects, even years after I first started!

One fine morning, a sweet lady gave us a buzz to book an appointment for her and her lovely daughter for the following week. They were keen to try out our heavenly facial and reflexology treatment. As soon as they arrived, we welcomed them with open arms and a hot cup of herbal tea. Let me call the mum "Mrs. A——" and her daughter "Debra" (for privacy reasons, of course!). We had a blast getting them pampered and chatting away. We covered everything from juicy gossip to their travel plans and overall health. It was an afternoon full of laughter and good vibes! As we chatted, Mrs. A mentioned her younger daughter who was no longer with them. Suddenly the room filled with a wave of sadness, and tears streamed down her face as I listened to her story. Just a few weeks before this appointment, Mrs. A's daughter had passed away, and their original plan was for the three of them to attend together to seek some respite and relaxation. It was heartbreaking to hear that the cancer that took her daughter was so aggressive and sudden. We delved into their treasured memories and how they yearned to explore new treatments, including reflexology. Spending time with the family was a roller coaster ride of emotions, from tears to belly laughs. Those moments will stay with me forever.

Sometimes life gives us a lightbulb moment where an idea or feeling becomes more important than ever before. That is exactly what happened when I had a heart-to-heart with this lovely family. It hit me that I needed to expand my caring and empathy for other illnesses, such as cancer.

Cancer talk is all around us, yet it is hard to grasp the impact it has on patients and their families. My curiosity led me to ask countless questions, such as "How did it start?" "Why did it happen?" and "What caused it?" It was surprising to hear people's first thoughts on the topic, such as "But she never smoked!" or "He was so healthy!" or "So young!" The more I dug, the more I realized there were too few answers. What is up with diseases, anyway? Why are some folks blessed with nothing more than a common cold, while others are thrown on a wild roller coaster of a journey? The questions kept coming, but the answers were harder to find. Ah, the age-old question: did we inherit our genes, or did our beliefs and lifestyles create our illnesses? This conundrum has been debated for ages, and I could not resist diving deep into books and research to assess my theories. How does asthma connect to eczema, and why does diabetes strike at any moment? So many mysteries!

After my practitioner course, I hungrily devoured two intense training seminars, eager to learn more. Anthony Lee Porter, a fantastic author and teacher, runs fantastic studies and courses on allergies and intolerances. He is based in the southwest of England. The awesome Suzanne Enzer runs courses in pregnancy and fertility. For me this included ten case studies over a six-month duration. I got to experience both the diabetic and cancer patients' clinics, and wow, it did shake me awake! The way we treat our bodies is like a wild roller coaster ride full of twists and turns. We never set out to hurt ourselves or our loved ones, but somehow sickness can sneak up on us. It is a whole new world of understanding, and its high time we take a closer look at how we can take care of our health. Sure, we can psychoanalyze every nook and cranny of our lives, but when we peel away the layers, we realize how our experiences shape us. For instance, losing a parent can affect kids in diverse ways. One may develop a serious condition, such as breast cancer, while another might have minor issues like voice or throat troubles. It is fascinating how our life stories are written on our bodies and minds!

Breast cancer, as just one example, may have a deep connection with grief that keeps the patient feeling stuck. On the other hand, the throat or voice can get all cranky and restless when you do not speak up about what is on your mind. Luckily, science has done a ton of legwork in these areas, helping us develop better treatments and diagnostic tests. And we would not be where we are today without them! While I am getting my treatments, I love chatting about the root cause of health issues, how they connect to the body, and ways to heal. Sometimes our conversations uncover buried topics that have never become exposed. It is funny how your feet always give away the secrets during treatment. They cannot keep a secret! But if you are not ready to release some trapped energy, that is cool too. Reflexology is not just about rubbing feet; it is a soulful experience that taps into the essence of my clients. I cannot stand it when people dismiss it as a mere foot massage; they are missing something incredible! During the treatment, my techniques and even my energy can trigger a deep release. It is common for clients to feel as if they have been hit by a truck—but do not worry; it is not as scary as it sounds. I prefer to call it a "release" because that is exactly what it is. It could be an emotional conversation or a flood of tears with a cathartic feeling of relief.

From stiff or sore joints to headaches, various individuals experience physical discomforts. As a primary treatment, I always recommend a reset or detox treatment to my new clients. It is imperative to drink water after the session, but I do not necessarily adhere to the trend of drinking ten glasses. Instead, I suggest having a few large glasses and gauging how one feels the next morning. People's water intake requirements are highly individualized; some may need more, while others may need to limit their intake. The following day serves as a beneficial reference point to record how one feels. If it turns out that one still has a headache, it indicates that an extra glass or two might help cleanse one's system in the hours to come. The reset button's effectiveness varies from person to person, but deep, restful sleep is often a common outcome, as well as increased awareness of how one's body functions.

The shop was buzzing with clients galore! Not only that, but I suddenly found myself catering to sports injuries and homebound clients. Sports injuries are serious business, especially when it comes to reflexology. Imagine an athlete with an aching shoulder. No problem! We can work our magic on the foot reflexes to ease the pain and speed up the healing process. Reflexology is like the fairy godmother of pain relief! Who said learning cannot be a blast?

I may not have kids of my own, but diving into the world of pregnancy and fertility was a real revelation. Over six months, I took on ten case studies, ranging from first-time mums to reflexology newbies. And let me tell you, the changes in their feet during pregnancy were mind-blowing! Who knew the incoming embryo had such a specific location on the reflexes? And do not even get me started on why it is a bad idea to buy shoes while pregnant (seriously, you will not believe it!). My time with these fascinating case studies even led me to help a couple who were headed to the fertility clinic. And the best part? I am still in touch with some of them, watching their babies grow into teenagers. Now that is what I call rewarding research!

CHAPTER 22

After graduating from a Scottish school, I lived a healthy life, but lupus still lingered in the background. I had to keep up with regular blood tests and kidney check-ups, especially after a biopsy revealed some severe damage. Back in 1983, the doctors gave me a gloomy forecast, saying I had only six years left. But fast-forward to 2008, and I was still here, kicking and fighting. That is why when I got that phone call, my world was shattered into a million pieces. Oh, the dreaded C-word—"Creatinine," that is! It is an annoying waste product from our kidneys, and the normal range is 60–110 units. But then, from out of nowhere, my consultant threw me a curveball: "Hey, you need to start thinking about dialysis methods, my friend." There are a few different dialysis options tailored to suit different folks. I must have looked like a deer in headlights, because I can barely remember what I said next. Shock, devastation, and fear flooded me all at once. I had a booming business and exciting plans on the horizon. But now my entire world felt as if it were crumbling down. It was not like I could just bury my head in the sand, right? Or could I?

The next few weeks of my life are a total blur. I cannot even begin to explain them. I had left everything behind—my clients, my staff, my entire business—and landed myself a job with Tui Travel in the Canary Islands. To be frank, I was ignoring the signs and living in my own little bubble. I felt fine, but my thoughts were starting to spiral. Ah, the good times! I was celebrating in Fuerteventura, working in the travel industry, and catering to La Carte clients. One moment, everything was dandy, and then *boom!* My friend found me sprawled out on my bathroom tiles. The ambulance whisked me off to the hospital, where some funky test results left the docs scratching their heads. My creatinine levels had increased very quickly, yet I felt strangely okay, despite shedding a ton of weight. It was like being in *The Twilight Zone*—no fever, sickness, or yellow skin tint typical of kidney or liver problems. The hospital urged me to stick around for dialysis, but I was having none of it, so I high tailed it back home. My company helped me dodge the chaos, and with some tough phone calls to my parents and consultant, I was set up with a hospital bed back home in the UK.

Upon my arrival, medical professionals drew my blood and informed me of a scheduled procedure to insert a neckline. I vividly recall tightly gripping the nurse's hand as the first local anaesthesia needle pierced my neck. A small incision was made about three inches below the shoulder in line with the breastbone, followed by a considerable amount of pushing and pulling that made it difficult to discern which was worse. The tube's insertion into the artery was especially painful, particularly as it drew closer to my heart. The sensation in my heart was almost ticklish; it was quite bizarre! A tiny tube was about to start my kidney journey, a doorway of opportunity leading to a life-saving procedure. In a moment, doctors opened a secret passage through my neck, allowing a dialysis machine to bypass my kidneys. The whole setup was like a fancy plumbing system with three tubes: one nestled in my artery, the other two snaking around my chest, connecting me to the machine. But ouch! My neck was screaming in agony, feeling like a battle scene with muscles torn and cut. Sleeping was a nightmare with that bulky plastic tube sticking out of my neck. If only I could sleep like an Egyptian mummy and not roll over on it! Even walking became a balancing act, as if I were carrying a precious vase.

The day after the line was put in, I sat there in my hospital bed, waiting for my ride to dialysis, feeling like a prisoner of plastic. The hospital hallways were buzzing with activity—nurses hustling to clock in, patients being wheeled around. As I made my way to the dialysis unit, the mood shifted. A serene silence surrounded the waiting area, where patients were quietly being called in for their treatment. As I stepped into the main room, rows of cosy recliners wrapped in crisp white sheets and pillows revealed themselves, waiting to cradle us during the long hours ahead. First things first, once I snagged a seat, it was time to hit the scales! Whether one strutted one's stuff or wheeled one's way in, the weight was a must-have for all kidney patients. Trust me; tracking your weight is vital.

At first, I was still doing the usual number one business (or so I thought), until I realized I was not hitting the mark. But no fear! The dialysis machine had my back and worked its magic, acting as my new kidney and filtering out all the gunk just like the authentic organ. Did you know that your kidneys work hard to cleanse your body in a twenty-four-hour cycle? But guess what—the machine can rock the same cleanse in just three or four hours! For those of us with kidney troubles, these machines are literal superheroes, keeping us going. As I faced my dialysis day, I felt as if I were stuck in a terrible dream. The chairs were a meaningful change, with armrests and remote controls that let me adjust my position from sitting to lying flat. I soon learned how to make the most of those reclining chairs and find my comfortable spot! Who wants to sit still for hours on end? Not me!

Every dialysis session kicks off with the crucial task of checking the patient's weight and blood pressure. These two little numbers can make an enormous difference! They give a peek into how the body is responding to treatment and whether the patient's meds are doing the trick or not. For renal patients, weight is important too. It is like a report card for how much fluid they have been hanging onto between dialysis sessions. So, I hopped on the scale and see what your body has been up to!

Here is the deal for dialysis patients: After a few rounds of treatment, the nurses weigh you to find your dry weight, which is your weight without extra fluid. Every time you eat or drink, your body stores the excess fluid, which can be a bummer if your kidneys are not working. Even simple pleasures like chugging your favourite drinks, munching on ice cream, or devouring a cucumber add to the fluid overload. But fear not! The machine tracks all the extra fluid, and the nurses will keep an eye on it throughout your treatment. As my kidneys slowed down, I had to dial up my dialysis and watch my fluid intake like a hawk. Eventually my kidneys admitted defeat, and I was told to hit up dialysis every Monday, Wednesday, and Friday. But here is the kicker: I was allowed only 750 ml of fluid in a day! And that included everything—even the milk in my tea and sneaky sauces that came with dinner. Talk about a liquid lockdown!

One of the few positive aspects of dialysis is the heavenly combo of warm cuppa and crunchy toast during morning sessions. It might sound odd, but hospital toast is like a slice of heaven. Plus, while you are hooked up to the dialysis machine, munching on snacks and sipping drinks will not count towards your daily fluid intake, since everything gets filtered out. During my early days on the machine, the food trolley rolled in, and I was warned to take it slow since snacking on the machine can make one feel queasy or dizzy. I remember having the tea and a couple of bites of toast. Then it was as if I was going deaf with extreme light-headedness. Everything went black! This is why the chair can recline. The nurses came and removed the tea and toast. My chair was pushed into its full tilt, where my head was much lower than my body, which in turn increased blood flow to my head. They amended some numbers in the machine, stopped the fluid removal, and gave me a little fluid back. As we eat, the brain sends a signal to the stomach to increase blood flow—all very clever! Whilst hooked to the machine, my blood pressure can take a nosedive, causing a momentary blackout—not the most chill experience. So, I have sworn off food and drink during the sessions.

The dialysis unit was a melting pot of ages and genders, from groovy thirtysomethings to hip octogenarians. Some had been visiting for years; others were still deciding between continued dialysis or, like me, waiting for a transplant. But what kept us all going was the amazing support from the staff and fellow patients. We shared tips and tricks and bonded over our respective struggles, proving that sometimes a little chat can be the best medicine. When I first started dialysis, it felt as if I were jumping through hoops in a circus! My body and the machine had to learn how to tango together, and it was not easy. I never knew what to expect, and sometimes I would get bizarre reactions without any explanation. One time, my face decided to puff up like a balloon, but it went back to normal once I was off the machine. Dialysis machines are like your trusty sidekick, taking over your body's duties, from regulating blood pressure to keeping those electrolytes in check. It is a wild ride, but we are in it together!

The machine was a marvel, with its blood-cleansing filter that made sure every drop of the red stuff in my body was as pure as freshly fallen snow. They were so meticulous in their approach that even the slightest hiccups meant they had to swap out the filter, thinking it was causing a reaction. It was as though the machine was tailor-made just for me, every setting calibrated to suit my body's unique needs.

With the neckline having been in place for ten months, it was time for my vascular surgery. Ah, the neck lines—a quick and easy dialysis fix but not exactly a long-term solution. My blood flow can get cramped and let me just say it caused me quite a few snags. So, the doctor suggested a fistula in my left arm. What is that? Well, it is basically when they join an artery and a vein to create a bigger, better blood vessel. No more neck lines sticking out like sore thumbs! The fistula hides under your skin, and it is all high-tech, with two needles doing the job on the machine. Way cooler, right? As I entered the operating room, I was initially anxious about the upcoming procedure. However, the friendly demeanours of the nurses and doctors helped to put me at ease. Thankfully, they opted for a combination of local anaesthetic and blocks, allowing me to remain conscious throughout the surgery. Despite my initial apprehension, I was feeling more comfortable and optimistic about the entire process. It took a few attempts to block the whole arm, but it soon was numb. I was watching in the large lights above my head as the first insertion on the side of my wrist was made as the procedure commenced. I was fascinated as I saw the skin open to display veins and layers of skin. It is not for the faint-hearted, but I was amazed by being awake and watching the surgeons going about this technique on my own arm. In a moment, the procedure was done and dusted, and before I knew it, I was back in recovery.

With the local block, my arm felt as though it had turned into a lead weight. I tried to move it, but it just plopped down to my side like a sack of potatoes! A few days later, I was back at the hospital for dialysis, and to my surprise, the healing process was coming along swimmingly! The bandages came off in no time, and I was on my way to speedy recovery. My superhuman healing abilities had seemingly kicked in again! The talks with the nurses and my consultant had covered getting a machine at home for dialysis in the future, so with this in mind, along with my new fistula, it was discussed that I would, once the fistula was mature, be learning to needle myself. It was a strange feeling when we discussed this, it was as though I knew I wanted to do it, but it was like, "How I can hurt myself!" I was experiencing very mixed emotions.

It would take six weeks for the fistula to mature. A normal-sized vein was now taking a larger amount of blood from the artery. As part of our regular routine, the nurses and I would regularly monitor the "buzz" of the fistula. During these checks, we would ensure that the fistula was healing correctly and that there were no signs of infection. The sound of blood rushing through the newly formed vein was reminiscent of a train speeding by. Once the fistula had fully healed, I would place it near my ears, and the rhythmic sound would lull me to sleep.

After six to seven weeks, the nurses informed me that they would attempt the new fistula. They began by listening to it through a stethoscope and then determining the location of the first of two needles. Like the neckline, the tubes regulated both arterial and venous blood supply, with one needle drawing blood from the heart and the other returning it, having been cleaned, back to the heart. Who knew that getting poked with needles could be a snoozefest? Unbelievably, I barely felt a thing! I mean, come on, it is a needle and my skin. But nope, not even a twinge. My doctor and I had agreed to stick to the same spot every time during dialysis, and it was a breeze. This process is commonly referred to as buttonholing, where the same entry point is used for both needles. After inserting the needles one by one, the syringe is placed on the needle, and once in the correct position, it is pulled to draw blood into it. This procedure confirms two things: the correct needle placement and the efficacy of blood flow. The process is painless both during needle insertion and after the blood is moved through the machine. Once the syringes are removed, they are attached to the machine, and the pumps are started and run for approximately four hours. Time to sleep!

CHAPTER 23

Throughout the period of 2009 undergoing dialysis, I experienced a combination of dizziness and weakness. My father would accompany me to the sessions to ensure my safety. During the treatment, my body resisted the procedure, resulting in fainting and other types of reactions. These reactions were more pronounced around the time when my neckline was used. However, as the weeks progressed, I began to feel a slight improvement in my strength. It is important to note that dialysis is a personal experience and every individual's body may react differently to the treatment. It is vital to become familiar with your own body and identify what works and what does not. I hold great admiration for the nurses and doctors who provided me with support during my challenging times. In such situations, it is imperative to recognize the significance of medical treatment; it is the machine that keeps one alive. Regrettably, not everyone has the privilege of experiencing this. As someone who enjoys inquiring, it is essential to comprehend what is occurring within and around my body. This, in turn, alleviates any concerns I may have.

During my reflexology training, I recall realizing that although we share common organs and tissues, their maintenance and function can differ significantly from person to person. It is essential to remain inquisitive and ask questions during medical appointments. While the medical profession is admirable, it is important to remember that not every case falls into the same pattern or protocol outlined in medical training manuals. My body's a mystery, and it likes to keep my med squad on its toes! They have their usual bag of tricks, but my body likes to say, "Not today, folks!" It will trigger anything from swollen joints and a puffy face to a surprise round of nausea or a fainting spell! It seems every appointment is a new adventure with no rhyme or reason. So, what do the docs say? "You, my friend, are a medical marvel!"

CHAPTER 24

As I started to maintain quite good health in 2010, I was asked whether I was considering being placed on the transplant list. Without hesitation, it was a yes; special days were organized for me and fellow patients to attend and ask questions about everything to do with the operation. Now, I must stress here that the list is not a list where candidates are placed in a numeral order; they are placed on there with all their details: blood type, tissue type, antibodies, and how well they are currently. The list covers the whole of the UK.

A telephone call can come at any minute, and that is when you run—well, make your way—to the local hospital. "It is a match"—that is what you need to hear. It is very much a double-edged sword, as it means someone has passed over to give you a chance at life. There's no warning at all if you are lucky enough to receive this call; however, your phone is always on standby.

As my energy started to increase, and I say this lightly, after I returned home, I would sleep for an average of four hours, and that is on top of the four hours of treatment. The ability to engage in activities after resting felt fantastic. Over time, my condition improved, and I could walk along the country lanes without getting exhausted. However, boredom eventually crept in. My brain started to get busy! "What can I do now?" was the question. I went all in with my inner hippie, dabbling in everything from tending to my friend's horse to concocting aromatic oils that would make my muscles sing. I am not one to sit still! I have learned to listen to my body's signals over time and give it the TLC it deserves. When I was undergoing dialysis, I had a secret plan of alternating work and rest periods. I never wanted to overdo it and make my body feel as if it were in overdrive. It is the only one I have, so I have to treat it right!

My helping with my friend's horse increased, and even though I never fancied jumping on board, I thoroughly enjoyed my equine visits. Anyone with a horsey background will understand this next statement: it is the horse smell, and I am not about the manure smell! Every horse has a unique smell; that is the connection! I do not recall my mind being made up on the issue of getting a horse. My thoughts were still up in the air about whether to buy a horse or not, but it seemed destiny had other plans for me in the days that followed. I came across a classified advertisement for a superior thoroughbred mare. Despite having no prior experience with such a high-performing animal, my acquaintances cautioned me about their temperamental nature, deeming them a potential risk. I thought I would see her and make my mind up. So, I went to visit the local farm where she was stabled. On arrival, I explained that I was a tad weak from some treatment, so I would not be riding. "No problem," said the owner; his daughter would ride. The horse, named Maisie, was in a very dark stable with no windows, and I remember thinking, "Gosh, she looks sad."

The young rider tacked up and mounted this beautiful, light bay–coloured mare. People, if you are not familiar with thoroughbreds, they are athletes and can come across on the lean side. This was true with Maisie. The young girl walked her down the yard, but it was not long till she was being beckoned back to the stable. Maisie was not allowed to go any further out in the yard, and she started to spin and rear. Oh, the joys! With that, I said I would take her! She was not happy here, and I knew fate had played a card here for some reason.

My decision to purchase Maisie was not made impulsively or without careful consideration. Despite any scepticism from others, I felt a powerful sense of conviction that it was the right choice. While it may appear peculiar to some that I would take on the responsibility of caring for a horse while still recovering my own health, the reality is that it was not a decision I took lightly. As I began to feel better, I faced a choice between seizing opportunities to live a fulfilling life or resigning to a sedentary lifestyle. It is easy to become overwhelmed by negative influences in our surroundings that can dampen our spirits, but I refuse to let that be my reality. Life is short, and we only get one chance to make it count. Maisie was delivered to a local yard a few miles from home. The cosy and chilled atmosphere of the yard seemed the perfect place for us to strike up a new companionship. The livery yard would be a nice, relaxed place for both of us to form a new friendship. There were other fellow girls with their horses who stayed in the yard too, which gave Maisie a new playground to explore. This she did, running around the paddocks with the other horses; these were ex-racehorses too. Maisie was around 16.1 hands high, so for me she was quite big! I seemed to like both larger dogs and horses, and to date I am a little wary of the small horses and dogs! Maisie had been bred to race, but it turned out she had not been fast enough. I am personally not a great fan of the racing industry and the months, and years that followed certainly did not alter my mindset.

Those winter months were a barrel of laughs, with frozen taps and snowdrifts to rival the Himalayas! Maisie and I were close, sharing laughter and making memories that lasted forever. She was one quirky gal, with a firecracker personality that matched mine. We were like two peas in a pod! I even gained a sense that she knew I was not 100 per cent healthy and was always so gentle around me. I would just stand by her side and place my hands either down her neck or on her back. The heat was amazing, and soon her head would drop, followed by licking or chewing action; it was just magic. The winter of 2010 was a very cold and snowy one; we had difficulties with water and snow for a couple of weeks. All the other girls would help each other out, especially if we could not make it to the yard to do our duties. As January lifted, there was a respite in the weather, and cosy nights by the fire were always on the cards. My health at this time was okay, nothing startling, but I was just in my element with Maisie to keep me going. With such a responsibility, I did not want to let her down.

February 5, 2011, was a normal Saturday, which I spent mucking out the horses. There was no turnout that day because of the weather; however, all was good in the yard. I would spend hours up there just pottering about and helping where I could. Hay nets were to be filled, water was to be collected, and feeds were to be prepared for the following day. During our daily duties, my gal friends and I were struck

104

with an idea to let us shake things up with a night out. And not just any boring night out—we are talking about dinner at a local pub!

As soon as the horses were tucked in for the night, we hit the road to change into our fancy clothes. Adventure awaits! Where my parents lived was just outside the town, approximately four miles; unfortunately, the mobile phone signal was not the best, so I quickly washed, dressed, and drove back into the town. As I parked my car, my mobile phone started to ring out. "Mother?" I spoke with a shaky voice, she replied, "Please hang up; the transplant coordinator is trying to contact you!" *What!*

I dropped the phone, and straight away the mobile rang again; when I answered, sure enough, the coordinator, Julie, asked whether it was me and said that they had a kidney match. "Please make your way to the Freeman Hospital Newcastle upon Tyne." Oh, my days. I thought my heart was going to jump out of my chest! I remember talking to myself in the mirror, telling my reflection all was going to be well. I also kept telling myself, "This is my new journey that awaits me." My biggest fear was getting put to sleep, which is nothing compared to a six-hour operation!

On my arrival at the hospital, Mum and Dad were on route, and soon my bags and I were heading to Newcastle. I called the girls from the yard to explain and ask whether they would look after my horse. "No problem" was the reply.

I was allocated a bed, and a series of tests began. Routine tests, such as blood pressure and pulse, were conducted, followed by an ECG to monitor my heart's rhythms. Subsequently, multiple bottles were filled with my blood for testing, despite my having received blood tests before. These tests were necessary to confirm my blood type and the presence of antibodies before proceeding with the operation.

After arriving at approximately 10.00 p.m I received the incredible news of the procedure's confirmation by midnight. It is worth noting that some individuals may not receive the green light, owing to incompatible blood tests or unsuitable donor kidneys. The operation was scheduled for the next afternoon. I had been informed that the donor's kidneys were both being transplanted. There was a male who was to be operated on first in the morning, then me around 4.00 p.m.

They also checked my abdominal area where the new kidney would be placed. They checked my blood flow from the femoral arteries that run from the kidneys down through the legs. They checked which side was the best regarding the blood flow. It was decided that the blood flow on the right -side was the best. After a large black marker pen was used on my right leg, I was all set.

Sunday morning was a blur, really. Plenty more tests were conducted, and I took in zero by mouth from 6.00 a.m.—no breakfast! The day itself went extremely fast with the normal comings and goings in the ward. The whole ward was geared for all kidney and pancreas transplants. I remember thinking, "Gosh, there are loads of transplants going on—a bit like a production line!" At approximately 4.00 p.m., a compassionate nurse escorted me to the operating room. The atmosphere shifted significantly as we proceeded to the anaesthesia room, which was much cooler. Here the Venflons were inserted into my veins to administer any necessary medication. The anaesthesia room was a remarkably busy room with an array of both machines and alarms going off intermittently.

During my dialysis treatment, my veins proved to be challenging to insert needles into, and unfortunately, this is still the case. Getting the needles into my veins on this Sunday again proved to be difficult. As I anticipated being put to sleep, I could feel my heart rate escalating. However, the nurses and anaesthetic doctors were incredibly supportive, offering reassurance throughout the process. Despite the process feeling like an eternity, I soon drifted off to sleep. The next thing I remember is being told I was back in recovery, and all went well. As I tried to open my eyes, I was feeling extremely dopy, but the nurse was by my side. I came out with, "Please, can you thank all the vets for their assistance in my operation?" "Well, Diane, I can assure you there are no vets present," replied the nurse amidst fits of giggles.

I tried to move, but my body would not have any of it. I did manage to reach down to feel my wound. I brushed my hand slowly over the right-hand side of my abdominal area, but to my shock and horror, I felt no wound. Slowly, I took my hand to the left, and there I felt the large bandage covering the left side. On my enquiring later that night, they advised me that on further inspection the left side was the better option. I really thought that they had cancelled the operation; your mind starts to run away with you when you are filled with drugs. Wires were visible throughout my body, primarily stemming from my neck, where medication was being administered. I also had a handheld pump beneath my hand for pain relief and a catheter in place.

Back on the ward, there was a steady flow of nurses, all checking observations and asking how I was feeling. I felt amazing, really. There was no pain, and I never once reached for the pain pump. The catheter bag that lay in a cradle on the floor was empty, whereas, on the ward, the other patients had urine in theirs. On inquiring about this matter, I was told the kidney was still sleeping, which can happen with some transplants. I was a bit disheartened to hear this news but was advised to give it time. The next few days were a bit of a nosedive because there was no kidney function and I had to have dialysis to clear the toxins from my system. I always try to look for the positives during grey days. I am not going to lie here; I could not see many. The day after the transplant, I received a text from one of the girls who was attending to Maisie. Laura worked at the local race yard near the town. It went something like this:

Hi Diane, hope you are feeling strong. Maisie is missing you loads, as we are, too. Just a thought for you, we have a beautiful grey mare coming up for adoption this week called Betty! See attached photo.

A stunning 16.2hh grey mare, injured due to racing. Oh, my days, this was the horse I had been on since childhood. There was no second guessing here. Without hesitation, I replied with "Yes, please." Now I knew I had to dig deep here and get this kidney working. The kidney was still sleeping on day seven. I was not in any pain but was feeling very deflated. I was having trouble sleeping during this time too, which was not helping the matter. I would tramp the corridors in the early hours, trying to lull myself to sleep or create a very tired body. The last few days of my first week were quite emotionally draining, as I thought that despite my having received this kidney, it was not for waking up. I went inwards for a brief time. This would have to be short-lived, and

I was not to give up. I had so much to do with the horses, and they needed me too.

As Betty was to have box rest for at least three months, there was a lot of convalescents between the pair of us! Remembering my reiki days, I decided to try to tune into my new kidney. I would hold my hands over the wound and pray to the universe. There were waves of energy moving around, and when my eyes were closed, colours started to emerge. The colours would be quite dark and hazy at first, but over hours, these changed to vivid bright lights. I remember thinking there was something happening, but I could not put my finger on it. Over the following days, I would sleep with a warm pack placed over the bandage, hoping that the warmth of the pack would just wake it up and still feel cosy! Then, on day six, there was a small amount of urine in the catheter bag. It was very bloody in colour, but it was there. Over the next three days, this increased, and soon I was emptying my bladder myself. The relief I felt during these days was immense; the connection I now felt with this kidney was something I had never felt before. When people talk about what it feels like to be gifted with the gift of life, there are not enough words to fully educate people. As I said earlier, this is very much a double-edged sword; in this case, a sixty-seven-year-old female had passed over and, as it turned out, donated all her organs for transplant. This lady and many others who donate their organs give people like me and others a second chance at life. Please sign the organ donation list and have the conversation *now!*

The girls back home had enough stories to make a blockbuster film, but something seemed off with my trusty sidekick, Maisie. She was uncharacteristically quiet, as if she knew I was on the mend and missing her. Soon Betty, a new member of our horse family, would be arriving. This former racing horse had some wounds that needed three months of rest, and that was the best way to ensure complete healing. The team at the yard were absolute pros, caring for my beloved horses like family. Leaving them in their capable hands during my two-week hospital stay wasn't easy, but they knocked it out of the park! After some further tests, I was ready to leave the hospital in Newcastle with a huge grin on my face. No more dialysis meant I could devour all my favourite foods, including chocolate, without worry!

After my surgery, something hilarious happened to my taste buds. I never really cared for crisps, but then I suddenly was a cheesy crisp monster! I would munch on those bags as if it were my job! Adjusting to the imposed restrictions can be challenging, but I recognized the importance of adhering to them to increase my chances of success. When the restriction on fluid intake was raised, I was initially hesitant. However, I quickly realized that this change was necessary for the proper functioning of my new kidney.

CHAPTER 25

The wound was healing well, with twelve staples all in place and secure for me to leave the hospital. I felt on top of the world, as though I were alive again. You really do not know how ill you are until you have been blessed with a new kidney. I must take the anti-rejection drugs for the rest of my life; this is a small price to pay to have my life back. On arrival at home, I rested when I needed to, but the horses were beckoning me. I was not allowed to drive for six weeks, so my parents drove me to the yard to see my Maisie and meet the new addition, our Betty. Oh, my days, these beautiful animals were just the tonic I needed. I really found it frustrating not being able to take part in stable duties. My body was alive, and I felt I could take on anything. My parents took me up to the yard every day for the next six weeks. Day by day, I started to increase some of the activities, such as hay filling and making feeds. Maisie was calmer than when I left for my operation. Betty was a beautiful dapple-grey mare; both her front legs were bandaged from the knee down to the ankle. These were to be changed every day, and a cold-water hosing down was to be administered if needed. As thoroughbreds are pure athletes, they find it hard to be stable for long durations without stretching their legs. My heart went out to dear Betty, stuck in her stable for the sake of her legs, but she was a trooper through it all. Luckily, there was a cosy little arena where Maisie could run free, and boy did she make the most of it!

As the six weeks of my rest were ending, my stamina increased, allowing me to muck out the stalls and walk Maisie down the country lanes. When thoroughbreds are put through their paces, they often train in pairs, and that was the drill for Maisie too. But boy, if I took her out solo, it would be a whole new adventure! She would stand still, then try her luck and not move forward without spinning around, refusing to continue with the morning walk. We would have a few cross words, but soon we would be on our way. Time flew by, and before we knew it, summer was here! Betty and Maisie were having a grand time nibbling on the luscious green grass. Their once-injured legs had recovered, and they bounced back with a spring in their step. I spent the summer pottering around the yard on sunny days, giving the horses good old wash-downs and tidying their manes and tails.

My health was feeling the love too! With every ray of sunshine, I felt like a sunflower reaching for the sky. Once I wrapped up my yard duties, I simply sunk into a cosy nook, soaking up the sunshine and feeling the good vibes. The upcoming months were like a school for our four-legged friends. Betty's legs were back in action, ready for some smooth rides, while Maisie had mellowed out since the first time we met.

As 2011 ended, we found ourselves at a crossroads with our dear yard. It was time to make a change to ensure our majestic horses had the best environment to thrive. After careful thought, we made the exciting decision to move to a new location.

The recently acquired location boasts a vast expanse featuring a diverse range of activities, including cross-country jumping, indoor show jumping, and local dressage events. Our backyard became the ultimate training ground for these majestic creatures, and boy oh boy, did we hit the jackpot! We were breaking new ground with our training routine, and it was a learning experience for both the animals and me. For two years, we had a total hoot trying out all sorts of exercises! My heart belonged to Maisie as we soared through cross-country jumps, but let me tell you, Betty was a dressage superstar! They took to their new routine very well.

Early spring 2014 was a busy time. Another phone call came in from the local racing yard. The phone call went something like this: "We have another horse who has been injured whilst out racing, and we wondered if you could take him." The details were made, and I now was the proud owner of Swallow, a huge 16.3hh dark bay thoroughbred. Oh boy, the ranch was full of life! Two mares and now a gelding. It was a party: Betty, my resident horse whisperer matriarch; Swallow, who would endure three months of box rest in his stable before getting back to work; and Maisie, who was watching over all closely. I was buzzing with life and feeling like a million dollars; giving back to those majestic animals was so fulfilling! It was as if I were in the best shape of my life, soaking up the moment and nurturing both them and I. Three months flew by, and soon the team was out grazing together. They were all great friends.

To keep the pennies rolling in, I was offering friends and family reflexology sessions. When I first came back to my work, I felt quite torn about splitting my time between the horses and my clients, but it had to be done. It was all about having a happy medium, along with it being very therapeutic for me too. Over the course of the subsequent two years, we relocated to a yard closer to our home and adopted a more relaxed approach to my reflexology work and the horses' exercise routines. This period served as an opportunity for us to reconnect and find a more harmonious balance in our lives.

Although filled with laughter, we could not avoid the occasional sombre moment. On a chilly autumn morning, my friend and I decided to groom our horses by clipping their coats. This event of clipping was well-attended by racehorse yard owners. It proved to be an effective way to maintain their horses' coats during the winter months, while also helping with warming routines. After the clipping process was finished, rugs were placed over their backs, and they were ready for an afternoon in the field. As I released them into the field, they immediately burst into a gallop, frolicking with playful abandon. After rolling about and kicking their heels up, they eventually settled down to graze. At this point, I walked back towards the stable block; I did not get in the gate before there was a mighty commotion of hooves and horses. On turning round, I met Maisie limping towards the gate. I could see the ankle joint did not look the best at all. As I opened the gate, she and the rest of the herd bounded straight back into the stables. I am not sure how it really happened; it was a bit of a blurry event. Maisie was in her own stall, sweating all over. The ankle was broken. Oh, my days. I went into a complete meltdown.

It is strange how things go into complete slow motion when we are around tragedy. I was a complete mess when they drove me home.

The vet was called, and Maisie was put to sleep. I sobbed and sobbed over the days that followed, experiencing a mixture of shock and total disbelief. Maisie was laid to rest in the field where the tragedy had occurred. For hours I sat on the newly turned earth where she lay. Having grown up in the countryside, I had always been privy to the natural cycle of life. The weeks that followed the tragic incident were a complete blur as I struggled to come to terms with what had happened while also trying to connect with the rest of the herd. The memory of the terrible accident still lingers with me today. Betty and Swallow were also deeply impacted by the event, sometimes avoiding escaping to the field altogether. The emotional toll we experienced was unlike anything we had ever felt before. I could not stand the thought of Betty and Swallow suffering; I would spend hours doing energy work over their backs and legs. They both enjoyed our treatment time, as did I.

I did not ride either horse for around three months; I became paranoid about letting them out or even riding them. During this time, I split my time between driving the lorries a few days a week and looking after the horses. Whilst I was waiting to load my lorry, my phone flashed up a message. It was listing horses for homes within the UK. Now, I hear you saying, "You do not need another horse!" Well, that is what my logical mind was also saying! One picture caught my gaze, and it was of a fine-looking ex-racer named Harry, a towering 16.3-hands-tall horse with a sleek, dark bay coat, residing in Northampton. The gravitational force I felt towards this noble creature was beyond measure! I read his profile repeatedly, thinking, "Nah, he's way too far out there." But then, one week later, I summoned my courage and dialled the owner's number. Before I knew it, I had a date to visit. I kept this adventure all to myself, even borrowing a friend's lorry. Hush-hush! Arrangements were made for Betty and Swallow to be looked at during my hours on the road.

On arrival at the smallholding, I was introduced to a lovely lady called Erica. I had not spoken to her much about my illness for fear she might think I would not be strong enough or similar. What met me was a lovely human who just wanted the best for Harry. Erica, being a lupus warrior herself, totally understood where I was coming from. Afterwards, we went out for a ride, and Harry was the epitome of a true gentleman. There were no unnecessary remarks, and he even loaded into the lorry without a fuss. At this time, Erica handed me Harry's passport. Each horse possesses a personal passport that includes critical details, such as the date of birth and bloodline. Racehorse passports contain supplementary information, such as the breeder's details and vaccination dates. I could not believe my eyes as I flipped through Harry's passport. It turned out his breeders were the same as Maisie's! What are the odds? It was as if the universe were conspiring to bring Harry into my life that day, with all the vaccination dates and breeder info falling perfectly into place. I got home late that day, Harry never put a foot wrong, and he was soon to meet the rest of the tribe. Three horses now felt right! Incidentally, three is my lucky life number. To get your life number, add your birthday digits together until you get a single figure.

For example, 01/12/1972 would be like $1 + 1 + 2 + 1 + 9 + 7 + 2 = 23$ then $2+3 = 5$

Driving lorries was my only way to pay for my equine family, so I split my time between driving and the odd reflexology client. I did not have much time for anything else. I enjoyed hacking the country lanes those days, as the team was complete. An old friend of mine approached me in late 2015 and asked whether I was still driving. I replied that I was but that I really had had enough of tramping the roads. It was time to kick my treatments into high gear full-time!

Over the course of the next year, I found myself overexerting and neglecting my physical well-being, resulting in significant weight loss and reduced opportunities to pursue my passion for riding. Unfortunately, it became necessary to downsize my equine circle, as sometimes one must make tough decisions to navigate life's twists and turns. Owning a grey horse had been my lifelong ambition, and Betty proved to be an exceptional addition. However, loading and transporting her in the trailer posed some challenges. Considering the circumstances, my friend in Yorkshire would be an ideal match for Betty. She would enjoy leisurely rides without the need for extensive travel. Ensuring her safety required the help of a local equine transporter, who collected and delivered her to Yorkshire. I was pleased to hear that in the weeks that followed, she became a great mum to the younger ponies. It turned out that after an animal communicator and I had a chance meeting, the lady explained that Betty had a middle ear imbalance; she also went on to describe her to a tee. She described her attitude to racing and explained that she was from France. Her racing name was Etoile Adentes, meaning "beautiful star." Betty lost her life in 2022 from a broken leg in Yorkshire—ironically the same injury as her mum.

CHAPTER 26

In 2016, my business was thriving, and I had a consistent flow of clients throughout the following months. During this time, I divided my time between taking care of my horses and providing reflexology services. My day typically started with the early-morning tasks of mucking out, feeding, and turning out the horses to graze in the field. Occasionally I would participate in small dressage competitions, which I found to be an enjoyable experience.

During a recent session with a new client, we discussed a nearby event focused on promoting wellness through a holistic approach. It had been some time since I had the chance to attend such a gathering. These events often highlight a variety of therapists offering talents such as reiki, massage, and Indian head massage. Moreover, the retail stalls present a diverse range of products, including crystals, handmade candles, and local produce. It is common to find mediums providing hand or card readings, adding to the unique experience. The event was in a small village hall–type building with an in-house cafe for the public to use when events were taking place. I ensured all my business cards and flyers were ready along with my reclining chair. The chair in question was a great purchase, made from soft seating that fully reclined so the clients' feet were in a prime position to work my magic. The hall was arrayed with local therapists and retail owners. Once everything was set up, the doors opened, and the public mingled around, looking for their twenty minutes of relaxation or retail therapy.

During this event, I met people who either were new to reflexology therapy or were trying my techniques. During the afternoon, while the hall still had a steady flow of people, a young female approached me inquiring about pregnancy and fertility reflexology. We talked intensely about the treatment, explaining that there is no scientific proof that it can help. Without further action, she was in the chair with her husband standing over us, listening intently to the conversation. The couple had been trying for a baby for a few months with no positive results. In previous consultations, I had enjoyed including the partners as much as possible; I found it quite interesting that maybe both parents were not reading from the same hymn sheet for assorted reasons. For example, Mum was ready to take the next step into motherhood and was filled with excitement and joy, whereas Dad was more concerned about his work commitments or even finances. We discussed everything reflexology, including talking together and what both wanted in their path together. My training in pregnancy and fertility covered relaxation and, more importantly, a hormonal balance. This had been a real game-changer in my training. The lady and her husband left the venue feeling relaxed, and she described a feeling like walking on air. The weekend was a real mix of emotions for me. Meeting new people and feeling as if I needed to extend my clientele were calling cards for me. However, I had to find a happy balance between the horses and my workload. I knew from previous months that it was paramount that my health came first. Rest, reflexology, and horses—but not in that order!

I kept the good vibes flowing with my mind and spirit events, all the way through 2016. The response was off the charts for both my business and personal well-being. I was riding high, balancing my horse duties and bringing in new clients like a boss. Things got even more exciting when I attended a new wellness fair and crossed paths with some amazing people. Fate, you sly dog! The fair was quiet, but then something magical happened. I met Louise, a local legend who had left everything behind to chase her dreams in Dubai with her husband and two boys. Louise was a teacher by trade, and I was so excited to hear her story.

CHAPTER 27

Let me take you back to when I was a sprightly twenty-eight-year-old, gallivanting around the world during my travel agent days. One of my most glamorous adventures was a trip to Dubai, so luxe it made my travel agent blush! The Burj Al Arab was the first seven-star hotel in the world, situated on its own island. The opulent suites feature floor-to-ceiling windows with gulf or city views; I have vivid recollections of the luxurious suite, with its elevated bedroom adorned with the finest linen. The decor was tastefully designed, complete with a study desk equipped with a fax machine and printers, ready to be utilized. The bathroom was an opulent marble masterpiece fit for royalty. What stood out to me was the exquisite fragrance emanating from the perfume bottle provided, which was unlike any I had ever smelled before. I recall feigning an upset stomach on one of the days to forgo the tour of the city, instead opting to relish the suite's amenities, savouring every moment. Oh boy, did I have a blast in Dubai! We went on a wild ride through the sand dunes in a fancy 4 × 4 and explored the gold and spice souks. The whole trip was a feast for the senses, with exotic smells and thrilling adventures that I will never forget!

During the event, Louise and I established a strong rapport. We even discussed the expatriate community in Dubai and how her acquaintances missed the personal and British treatments offered there. She remarked that numerous therapists or spas there lacked an individualized touch, appearing to go through the motions. Louise mentioned that it would be a fantastic opportunity if we could arrange to offer our services in Dubai to the expatriate clientele, many of whom work in schools or reside in the vicinity.

I must put my daydream mind aside temporarily, as fate intervened that day. That day was a ray of new people relaxing on my reflexology chair. My next chance meeting was a lady around the same age as me. A beautician with a vast array of therapies under her belt. I do have a slight pet hate here when it comes to beauticians practising reflexology. Throughout my reflexology exam preparations, I realized the significant investments of both time and money that were required to practice this truly amazing therapy. It is not just a foot massage! Conversations with fellow reflexologists corroborated this notion, as many expressed similar experiences. However, there is a growing trend of quick, condensed reflexology courses available to the masses, such as those included in beautician courses. During the beautician's reflexology session, I clarified that I typically do not take consultations and prefer to work solely on the soles. She agreed to proceed with the "taste" session in the same manner. As I began to work on her feet, I noticed some imbalances and blockages. While we chatted about diverse topics, she gradually began to relax, and the session confirmed the alignment of her body and mind. Meet a beauty queen with more than twenty-five years of experience who has even travelled the high seas with her magical touch! The beautician was intrigued by my reflexology and invited her friend to join in on a taster sesh. As we chatted away, during this time she disclosed information on her new salon, which was just a hop and a skip away from the venue we were at. Our discussion centred around visiting the salon to assess its viability for my reflexology. After a few weeks, we held the meeting, and it was unanimously agreed that the salon would be an excellent fit. Initially we planned to start with one day per week, with the possibility of expanding based on the demand. I was all set to take my business to the next level, and the energy just felt oh, so right!

A few days later, fate was still dealing the cards. I got a bunch of messages from Louise asking whether I had any extra thoughts about travelling to Dubai. I honestly thought they had been passing comments. *My days. Dubai. Why not!*

I searched the Internet for flights and discovered that Emirates provides flights from Newcastle, which is a short drive from my location. Louise suggested that I could stay with her family and help arrange meetings with potential clients. The number of clients increased thanks to Louise and word of mouth. I still have lifelong friends in

Dubai, and I am forever grateful for my opportunity to spread the word about reflexology. Every six weeks, I would pack my bags and hit the road for ten days of adventure! But I never forgot about my trusty steeds and made special arrangements for them too. Despite the occasional wave of fatigue, I was surprised to find myself thriving in the new weather conditions. But let us be real, even I needed a breather from the sweltering heat of July and August; it was the locals' favourite time for vacationing.

As I went about my trips, I was greeted with nothing but wide smiles and open arms, thrilled that I was practising my little reflexology business in Dubai. It was a total culture shock! I mean, the last time I came here was during my travel agency days, and it had been over twenty years since then. Now Dubai was a whole new universe! The coast was now a glittering skyline of colossal hotels and megaplexes. The roads were like a wild, twisting ride, bigger and crazier than any roller coaster I have ever seen!

I spent an incredibly happy time in Dubai with exciting new people and their soles!

Back in the small salon, which was in the small market town in Cumbria, work was steady, mixing both horsey life and my reflexology. Our work was a seamless blend of reflexology and massage. We collaborated to offer our clients the best in holistic health, with a double clinic approach that provided an hour of reflexology followed by a full-body massage. This approach proved to be highly effective in treating complicated health conditions. During the session, I would identify noteworthy areas that required attention, which she would adjust her massage technique to address imbalances noted during my reflexology treatments, leveraging our expertise to target stubborn areas and achieve balance in the body.

CHAPTER 28

Now, reading this, I bet you're thinking, "What was next on the old fate line?" Well, 2017–2018 was a year full of surprises, and they kept coming.

My Scottish friend took me on a journey across the border to the charming town of Kelso. It is a quaint and snug location, steeped in history that spans centuries, encompassing everything from legendary rugby players to breathtaking country estates. It has been said that Kelso is the most architecturally attractive of the border towns. It is home to the largest market square in Scotland, with a cobbled area, imposing town hall building and Italianate coaching house, giving an almost continental feel.

A wonderful place to call home, the town of Kelso and its surrounding district is brought to life with a sense of community spirit based around work, home, school, sport, charity, church, and local celebrations. During my walk around Kelso, I came across several health food shops and beauticians, but I could not find any listed reflexologists. This sparked an idea, and I decided to visit a health and wellness shop located just off the high street. Upon my arrival, I was greeted by the friendly owner, Tracey. I inquired about renting out a spare room to practise reflexology once a week, and to my delight, she welcomed the idea with enthusiasm. Kelso was an unbelievably valuable addition to my ever-growing practices. Picture this: my calendar was bulging like a balloon. Brampton in Cumbria now needed me two days a week, Tuesdays and Thursdays, while Kelso gobbled up my Fridays. Before I knew it, I had a bonus Saturday up for grabs! My days hopping from Brampton to Kelso were a blast, with fresh and familiar faces streaming in every week.

My pets were living a comfortable life, with warm beds and an ample supply of hay to keep them relaxed during winter. In the spring, they had the liberty to indulge in grassy areas as much as they pleased. During those crazy busy times, I would often get a helping hand when running behind schedule, which was a major lifesaver!

May 2018 was a thrilling month, as I had an action-packed trip booked in Dubai with my clients. We were all set to rock 'n' roll for seven days of adventures before the holidays would commence. The horses were all catered for, and the diary for Brampton and Kelso was placed on hold till I returned. Off I jetted. What a week! I squeezed in some sightseeing, and I even got lost in the vibrant gold and spice souks. I am immensely thankful for my time spent in Dubai and for Louise, who paved the way for me. In my last few days there, while conversing with clients about India, the topic of Ayurveda emerged. If you are new to Ayurveda, this is a minefield of information. I have long held a profound interest in the study of the science of life.

CHAPTER 29

The idea of living and working in harmony with nature resonates with me deeply. By exploring both our inherent characteristics and environmental upbringing, we may potentially minimize illness and achieve a more harmonious existence. One of my clients had recently joined a detox and healing week and could not stop raving about the experience.

Upon returning to my accommodation, I utilized Google to search for the venue where my client had stayed. I started off with one fascinating article, and before I knew it, I had fallen into a rabbit hole of endless clickable gems, all leading to the same topic. There are several Ayurvedic schools that offer courses, and one of them had a six-month programme starting in June. The course offered the added benefit of a one-month trial period, allowing me to evaluate my interest in the subject. My head was now in overdrive! I had to become organized and wrangle up my thoughts, my responsibilities, and my trusty steeds back at the ranch! I reached out to all parties, Tracey, and Lucy and the beautician, who had agreed to care for the boys, outlining my desire to pursue my dream while I had the opportunity. I completed all necessary arrangements for my work and the boys for the next four weeks. The flight duration from Dubai to India is approximately three and a half hours, with a one-hour or so train journey to Kannur in Kerala.

Life's an adventure, and sometimes you must grab the bull by the horns and enjoy the ride! Life can be a wild ride, with surprises around every corner. But do not fret! If destiny has something in store for you, it will come knocking at your door. So, hold tight and enjoy the ride!

Kochi airport was a hub of activity, with a flurry of travellers, bags, and more travellers! I survived the train journey, and I was soon welcomed to the accommodation associated with the school. The ground level of the house comprised twelve bedrooms, each with an en suite bathroom. Upstairs, the expansive open-plan area boasts a stunning ocean view. The small kitchen was adequately equipped to prepare meals. The school provided a daily bus service to transport us to our lessons, while the weekends were left for us to explore at our leisure. During the first few days, we all shared information on our very varied backgrounds. Our group consisted of individuals with diverse backgrounds, including musicians, doctors, and travellers. During the initial consultation with the doctor, a comprehensive evaluation of the patient's physical constitution or body type was conducted, considering various aspects of his or her health and well-being. This involved a meticulous analysis of the patient's tongue and pulse to arrive at an accurate diagnosis. After diving into the world of Ayurveda, we were hooked! The first month breezed by as we soaked up all the juicy details about this ancient practice.

As we wrapped up, we found ourselves chatting about a return trip. The endless cravings for more knowledge kept our minds buzzing! The journey back home was a whirlwind, as my mind was preoccupied with various thoughts regarding my horses and work, both of which I have invested my heart and soul into. The thought of missing this opportunity recurred frequently, and the possibility of falling ill was always at the back of my mind. Living in this constant state of uncertainty felt like walking on a tightrope, and the memories of being unable to perform everyday tasks still haunted me. Was I to live life always wondering "What if …?" or was I to take a chance? The latter was my decision. I knew I had to do this, even if it felt like a testing time.

The next weeks were trying, a time in my life that took years to recover from. Upon my return to my horses, I noticed that Swallow, the younger one, had experienced some bleeding from a sarcoid that had been previously treated several years ago. Fortunately, there is a minimally invasive procedure that involves tying the root of a tumour, which is no thicker than a strand of hair. Over time, the tumour will naturally die off and fall away. However, if the root is not tied closely enough to the underlying cause of the tumour, it may regrow. Unfortunately, this was the outcome of a returning tumour that appeared between the back legs vigorously. The veterinary surgeon was immediately contacted, and an extensive assessment was conducted. Owing to the tumour's location, chemotherapy cream was not a viable option, as it would damage the unaffected side of the other leg. It is with a heavy heart that I must share that Swallow had to be euthanized. There was no other viable alternative, and I regret that there was no simpler way to deliver this difficult message. Anyone with animals knows that they are part of the family, and my boys have seen me through the most challenging times in my life. Swallow had the best life, and for that I am truly blessed. The subsequent days proved to be painful for both me and my beloved horse Harry. The sadness was palpable in Harry's eyes, and he did not even finish his evening feeds. His demeanour was understandably grumpy. I tried all sorts to help him without avail.

Two weeks later, I received a call from the yard stating that Harry had gone down with colic. Colic is a blockage in the intestinal tract, sometimes life-threatening. The vet can administer certain drugs or liquids to get things moving. On this occasion, nothing more could be done for Harry. In just two weeks, I lost two of my trusty steeds. I never saw that curveball coming! To clear my head, I hopped in the car and drove for an hour, then walked and walked, lost in my thoughts. The following week was a blur, and I found myself plagued with uncertainty about my future. Thoughts raced through my mind regarding my next steps and the actions I should take, leaving me feeling overwhelmed. I proceeded to pack my horses' belongings and stored them in my parents' garage. Surprisingly, despite the emotional turmoil, I found myself unable to cry, which only added to my sense of bewilderment.

I pondered the possibility of embarking on a journey and wondered whether fate had predetermined my travels to India. Conflicting thoughts and concerns surfaced. How would it impact my valued clients and potential business opportunities? Equally important, how would it affect my personal well-being? These factors all contributed to my current predicament. Upon reaching out to a former classmate, Nina, a beautiful soul originally from Paris, I discussed my circumstances. She expressed that not only was this a unique opportunity, but it could also serve as an added resource in my professional toolkit. After considering her input, I decided to return to India and complete my diploma in

Ayurvedic medicine. Following several phone conversations, I finalized my plans.

I stumbled into Kerala a dazed and drained traveller, but I was determined to follow my dreams. The Ayurvedic school was a buzzing hive of activity, with fresh-faced students and wise old owls alike, all ready to soak up the secrets of this ancient science. The first fortnight was a whirlwind of plant info, hands-on practice, and a deep dive into the art of body cleansing. My head was spinning like a top, but my heart was ablaze with passion for this knowledge. Unbeknownst to me, the process of my training had a significant impact on my emotional well-being.

During our first-hand training, we examined the practice of Shirodhara, which is a beautiful, relaxing, and calming treatment. In this treatment, you are placed on your back on a *droni* table, which is a hand-carved single piece of medicinal wood from the neem tree. A copper vessel hangs above your head, filled with either medicated oil, buttermilk, or cow's milk infused with herbs. As discussed prior to my consultation, the time had come for me to experience this treatment myself. The first treatment to be used was cow's milk and herbs. Now, I'm no wimp; however, I do not like the cold. *How am I to enjoy this?* I wondered.

Fast-forward sixty minutes, and I was getting woken up. I had been fast asleep. I'm not sure how that happened, but it did! I made my way back to the accommodation for a relaxing night. After a hot shower, I was lying on the top of the bed, resting, when, from out of nowhere, tears ran down my face, and they did not stop; in fact, they ran and ran for fifteen hours on and off. I have never experienced anything like it. The next day, I tried to pull myself together but ended up walking out of the lesson in floods of tears. I knew about backed-up emotions from reflexology training, but I never thought of myself with such emotion. Speaking to the doctors, they confirmed that such treatments can release emotions that can be deep-rooted. I was sure this was the trauma of losing my two horses. This experience has been a valuable lesson for me, and I spent some quiet time reflecting on the previous few years. I have had many treatments, but none quite as calming as these. The Shirodhara experience was the ultimate relaxation, like a river of warm, medicated oil cascading over my head. It is like the cow's milk ritual but with oil instead. The steady stream trickles over your forehead, easing from side to side, making its way through every strand of hair and into your scalp. Pure bliss!

As the end of November approached while we were busy preparing for our final exams, the previous five months seemed to have passed by quickly.

I am scratching my head, trying to figure out how the next chapter unravelled—if "unravelled" is even the right word! All my classmates, especially Isa, a gregarious girl from Maderia, and Rajeev, who was full of Chicago and Indian wisdom. We were chattering away about our next moves; some were jetting back to their homelands, while others were off on wild adventures to other exciting places in the world. Feeling stagnant and uncertain of my next direction was impulsive, but an intense longing to explore new horizons and spread my wings had always been a deep-seated aspiration. With so much on offer, I consulted the flip of a coin: heads, back to the UK, and tails, eastbound! Tails it was!

I recall snuggling up and watching my all-time favourite film *Eat Pray Love*. It is a heart-warming story of a woman, played by the mesmerizing Julia Roberts, who is clueless about her life, her marriage, and her very existence. The scenes where Julia jets to Italy, India, and Bali to find herself struck such a chord with me that this became a life goal. I really could see myself in this film, although I was not going through a divorce! I booked a three-week stay in Ubud, Bali, staying in a traditional-style Indonesian home. Ubud is famous for handicrafts, lush green tropical jungles, terraced rice fields, and Hindu temples and shrines; an Ubud holiday shows you the most authentic part of Bali in the best way possible. Shopping, temple hopping, and coffee tasting are just a few of the unique things to do in Ubud. This location is perfect for sightseeing and relaxation, with an array of amazing spa resorts nearby. Breakfast was served on the upper balconies, providing a picturesque view of the surrounding rice fields in the distance.

I teamed up with a savvy local guide who whisked me off on a wild adventure through the mesmerizing Tegalang rice terraces, with some epic swings thrown in for good measure. Next stop? The Pura Tirta

Empul temple complex, where holy spring water bubbles up from the earth, ready to work its magic. Locals and tourists alike flock to these waters, hoping to soak up some of the healing powers and take a dip in the cleansing pools. One of the interesting activities I did whilst in Ubud was a silver ring-making workshop. Now, I must confess I am not that nimble with making anything; however, the workshop was a day full of laughter. Here is the story: I met a charming lady all the way from Manchester, UK, now living it up in Sydney. Vicky and I hit it off like peas in a pod, giggling away as she filled me in on her wild past in Manchester. As the chat flowed on, we got down to business, and I shared my passion for reflexology. But it did not stop there; I said I had just come back from India and was itching for more adventures. "The world is our oyster," she replied. We chatted about home life, and she mentioned her daughter's Pilates instructor. She was always on the lookout for therapists who need a quiet space, so it seemed like a perfect match if I were visiting Australia. Names and addresses were swapped, and I would be made more than welcome anytime.

In Ubud, the people are always full of smiles and laughter. I joined the wild laughter on the breakfast balcony, relishing the taste of a fresh smoothie packed with delicious local fruits. Coral was a bubbly American gal who had just landed and was spinning the globe to plan her next escapade. I happily shared my travel tales and top picks with her over breakfast. We talked about travel and what we each had planned. I recall one of my last breakfasts we had together when she relayed a dream she had of me. Picture this: I was about to hop on a plane to Perth, Australia, and what happened next left me gobsmacked! The universe was playing a game of connect-the-dots with me, linking every little thing to Perth! From song lyrics to overheard yoga chatter, it was as if Perth was calling my name. Could it be a sign? Oh, I was sure of it!

My eyes were glued to my phone's flight app, hunting down any Perth-bound flights. I mean, who knew what kind of wild adventures were waiting for me on the other side of Australia? I booked a flight to Perth. Just a day before take-off, the airline hit me with a bombshell: the flight was cancelled! My mind was blown. But hey, the universe had bigger plans for me, right? I figured, "Let's try this again!" and I reached out to Isa, who was now exploring the wonders of New Zealand. After a quick chat, she revealed that she was now living it up in a charming village called Ragland, nestled in the heart of the North Island. With no dilly-dallying, she ordered me to make a beeline for Auckland. With just a quick bus jaunt, she promised to scoop me up. Oh boy, was I over the moon about the big trip! I got down to business and sorted out the details quickly. First stop: Auckland. I booked that flight in a moment! Then, come February, I would be off to Sydney with Vicky. I could not wait for the adventure!

I landed and quickly booked in a sweet Airbnb in the heart of the city. Ready for my next adventure, I hopped on a bus and headed south the following day. Raindrops danced down the windows of the bus on that chilly December day it wasn't long until I arrived in Hamilton, ready to brave the elements and wait for Isa. In no time, we were as thick as thieves, giggling away about the fantastic adventures we would have. Isa had been in Raglan for about a month and played tour guide, showing me the coolest cafes and shops in town. Nestled forty-eight kilometres west of Hamilton, New Zealand, lies the charming coastal hamlet of Raglan, a mystical land where the untamed west coast beaches, adorned with glimmering black iron sands and roaring surf, beckon visitors from afar. Raglan is the birthplace of New Zealand's surfing culture, where the spirit of wanderlust echoes is the town motto. For those seeking adventure, testing oneself against the surf is a must-do in Raglan. Nestled along the shimmering shores, a paradise for Hamiltonians beckons, whispered in the breeze of the ocean's embrace. Yet beyond its allure as a seaside retreat, this town has long been a sanctuary for those who chase the waves, with a surfing culture stretching back to the 1960s. Once known as Whāingaroa village, the sands of time shifted its name to honour the valiant Lord Raglan, commander in the Crimean War, in 1858. Amidst this coastal haven, Eva Rickard stands tall as one of the most vocal champions of Māori land rights, her words and deeds shaping the landscape of the 1970s. But Raglan is more than just a surfer's paradise; it is an art lover's haven, where the creative community thrives alongside a vibrant food scene fuelled by local ingredients. Visitors can relish the bustling art scene supported by local weekenders and indulge in a gastronomic journey that will tantalize their taste buds. For non-surfers, there are still plenty of activities to partake in, such as fishing, kayaking, or experiencing the tranquil beauty of stand-up paddleboarding. Shortly after my arrival, Isa introduced me to a woman who had recently relocated to Australia. She was selling assorted items, including her VW beetle. In New Zealand, the most convenient modes of transportation are either camper vans or cars.

Raglan is a town known for its transient nature, with people coming and going frequently. From the outset, the town felt incredibly open to me. After four days of being there, Isa and I explored the prospect of purchasing the car from the lady relocating along with a recliner chair, which would enable me to practise reflexology on a mobile basis. Isa posted a brief message on Facebook advertising the availability of mobile reflexology sessions provided by a Scottish girl in town. Although I had just lived in Scotland myself, I was astonished to receive numerous text messages within hours of the post. It was humbling to receive such an overwhelming response from people I had no prior connection with, and it was an honour to be invited into their homes. With the influx of messages and inquiries, my December diary quickly filled up.

Covering Raglan and surrounding areas, I set out with my reliable new car and reflexology chair. Meeting incredible people along the way, I learned a great deal from each encounter. Their vast knowledge included the history of the area, the Māori tribe, and much more. During my unforgettable weeks in Raglan, I met a true gem of a lady named Annie. She was a local legend who had lived in the town her entire life with her daughter and extended family. Annie reached out, and we set up a meeting that I will always cherish. Several appointments were made, including ones for her visiting daughter from Melbourne and even her ex-husband, who had travelled down from Auckland. Oh, what a chat! It was one of those unforgettable moments where we talked about everything from reflexology to the vivid life in Raglan versus the Scottish homeland.

Next up, I met with Annies's daughter, who came to visit her during the festive season. Her daughter had been living in Melbourne for a while now, where she had blossomed into a Pilates queen, running her own business like a pro. As I chatted about my plans to fly to Sydney in February and meet up with my friend, she suggested, "Why not rent a room within the studio and show off your reflexology skills there too?" Suddenly it felt like déjà vu all over again. *Pinch me, am I really living the dream?* I thought to myself as I mingled with all these kindred spirits. It felt as if fate had brought us together! Annie's ex-hubby was also in town for the holidays, now a true-blue Aucklander. Surprisingly, he had a few appointments lined up with me. This made me realize that guys, too, are embracing the natural way of health and wellness.

December was an action-packed month of fresh faces and an absolute tidal wave of reflexology love! Isa and I are total road trip junkies! We live for the sea breeze and sandy beaches, especially over the holidays. Our latest escapade took us to the stunning Coromandel Peninsula. From belting out car karaoke to gawking at jaw-dropping views, we zigzagged through winding roads that looked like a film set. We even snoozed in the car and went on a quest for secret treasures, and boy, did we find them, hiding around every bend! Life is a mystery, full of surprises around every bend. Who knows what amazing adventures are in store for us. We just must go and enjoy the ride! Several days following Christmas, I began experiencing symptoms akin to a cold, such as excessive sweating and joint pain. Consequently, I took a brief hiatus from work. However, as my condition did not improve, I opted to visit a nearby clinic for a blood test. Upon arrival, a friendly local woman greeted me and collected my personal information, as well as details of the medication I was taking for my transplanted kidney. During our conversation, we discovered that her daughter had lived in my hometown of Hexham while attending the Newcastle University Newcastle upon Tyne, UK.

What a quirky little planet we inhabit! As she handed me my results, she popped the question, "So, do you know how all this works?" Without hesitation, I answered, "Yep, I'm a pro!" She replied, "Your kidney function has significantly increased. Upon further examination, the test results indicate a creatinine level of 870, which is significantly higher than the average level of approximately 125. Hey, do you happen to have medical insurance?" I sighed. "Well, even if I did, I doubt it would cover any kidney mishaps." While I acknowledge the importance of travelling with insurance, I also recognize that in situations that require intensive medical treatment, being only a flight away can be advantageous.

After thanking the lady, I immediately headed back to Raglan, unsure about what to do next. I then drove to Isa's place to update her on the situation and discussed that it would be best for me to fly straight back to the UK. She agreed with my decision. As I gathered my belongings, I found myself overwhelmed with a sense of dread, aware of the potential consequences if my kidney had reached the end of its lifespan. The memories of past health issues, including fainting spells, sickness, and frequent hospital visits, came flooding back to me. Overcome with emotion, I hastily packed my clothes and sat down to process my thoughts. I could not help but wonder what lesson I was supposed to learn from this experience and why it was happening now, when I thought I had everything figured out. I contacted the clients who had made reservations in early January to inform them of my unfortunate decision to return to the UK. While at a local restaurant, I spoke with Annie, who was working that morning. I shared details of my recent visit to the clinic and let her know that I had already booked my flight back home. During our conversation, I expressed my sole concern—the safety of my vehicle. When asked by Annie if I wished to sell the car, I agreed that selling it would be an ideal solution. Annie suggested that her husband, Glen, could potentially assist me, as he was searching for a second car. A few calls to Glen were made, and he agreed to buy the car. It was to be arranged that I would leave the car at the fuel station next to the airport and he would collect it the next day. This was a huge relief as I said my goodbyes to the friends, I had made in the six weeks I had been in Raglan. Soon, I left for Auckland airport.

I left the car, as arranged, at the fuel station, and I soon was checked in for my thirty-six-hour flight back to Newcastle UK airport. I really do not remember much about the flight home; Emirates is an exceptional airline, offering food and drinks throughout the flight. I slept most of the flight while watching a movie at intervals. There was a quick stop in Dubai before the final leg. I relayed my whole journey in my mind—the action-packed highs and now this low. I could have never imagined this at any point during my whole year. When I look back in hindsight, given all my health concerns, I see that it would have been reasonable for me never to have left in the first instance. But hey, I had no regrets at all; I couldn't put my life on hold with what-ifs and so on. The universe had my back, and my path was to turn on a sixpence for a reason. I certainly was not going about my life being wrapped in cotton wool; I knew I had to travel to gain some valuable lessons on the way, which is worth every minute. The experiences, memories, and people who made that year were priceless, and with thanks, I am profoundly grateful.

CHAPTER 30

A lesson for everyone out there. I had phoned my parents before my departure to Auckland, and arrangements had been made to collect me and attend the local hospital in Carlisle, UK. Arriving back in the UK in January was freezing and a huge shock to the system. More shocks were to follow my arrival at the hospital, as I was soon to discover. I was met by my consultant, who commented on how well I looked; I really felt amazing and certainly did not feel as if my kidney had failed. Blood tests were taken and sent straight away to the lab. My bed awaited me on the ward, where observations commenced; blood pressure, pulse, and oxygen levels all were in perfect range. X-rays and CT scans were all completed; I remember one of the consultants who performed the CT scan telling me, "Loads of life left in that kidney." Oh, how wrong he was. The kidney function was confirmed, and as a last-chance saloon, I was attached to a drip with steroids flowing through my veins. During the time the fluid entered my bloodstream, my memories flooded back to my early days of medication, where these drugs sent my body and me into psychosis. It is not a great memory.

The final conversation regarding my kidney function was relayed to me two days later, when they had executed all options to save it. It was a shock to all concerned, and I knew what lay ahead for me: the part-time job of visiting the hospital three days a week, the neckline having to be inserted again, and the pain of being on a fluid restriction and not forgetting the foods that were to be avoided. The team looking after me was amazing as always; they were sorry to see me back in the dialysis unit. The days that followed were a complete haze, and if I am honest, I really nosedived for the first time in years. I completely went inwards. I went from buzzing about my escapes, the serendipitous moments that were amazing, to complete depression. I closed my bubbly nature to everyone from the nurses to my family. I knew I was not in the right frame of mind, but I really could not do anything about it. I was sleeping the whole duration on the dialysis machine; the neckline was sore and continued to cause the machine to alarm. The blood flows that were removing my toxic blood were not flowing to their full advantage, making me feel shaky and tired. I did manage to drive myself a few weeks later; I had few or no conversations with close family members, and even my consultant was taken aback by my attitude. Medications were analysed and monitored as the treatment continued.

The days soon turned into weeks, and by May 2019, I was pulling myself through this flow of treacle. I decided to try to return to work in Brampton one day a week. Thursdays would be a godsend, really; I needed to place all my remaining energy into people who really needed me; I needed to occupy my mind in a more constructive fashion. This was to be a catalyst going forward and how I needed to continue with kidney failure. There is one thing I have learned since that first day back on dialysis: you really must work with your body; you cannot fight this at any cost.

The dialysis was rubbish. Looking back over the few months I had been home, my clearance, which is measured after every dialysis, indicated how efficiently the machine was in cleaning my blood. During dialysis, the blood is filtered and cleaned before it is returned through the patient's veins, doing the job of the patient's own kidneys. It will never replace the function of one's own kidneys, but it can keep one alive, and for me that was paramount. I really had to keep that my priority.

As the months swept by—and boy, they seemed to—I needed to spread my wings regarding moving out of the family home. A very good friend of mine, Beverley, with whom I had struck up a friendship not long after I qualified in 2004, had been attending regular reflexology sessions with me, and we remained close friends. Back in the days of Fuerteventura, Beverly and I spent two weeks holidaying in 2010 when I needed to recover some personal goods after I had to leave because of my first kidney failure. Beverley's conversation couldn't have come at a more perfect time. She advised me that the small bungalow that her husband owned in Lockerbie was coming up for rent. Lockerbie is a town in Dumfries and Galloway, south-western Scotland. It is about 120 km (75 mi) from Glasgow, and 25 km (16 mi) from the border with England. Lockerbie is known internationally as the place where, on 21 December 1988, the wreckage of Pan Am Flight 103 crashed after a terrorist bomb on board detonated. In the United Kingdom, the event is often referred to as the "Lockerbie disaster" or the "Lockerbie bombing." Eleven residents of the town were killed in Sherwood Crescent, where the aircraft's wings and fuel tanks plummeted in a fiery explosion, destroying several houses and leaving a large crater, with debris causing damage to other buildings nearby. All 259 people on the flight also died. The 270 total victims were citizens of twenty different nations. The event remains the deadliest terrorist attack and aviation disaster in Britain.

The bungalow was centrally located in the small town, with easy access to the shops, the doctor, and the main carriageways linking larger towns and cities. I stayed in the bungalow for twelve months. Once I had moved to a different area, I had no option but to move to a different hospital. My new hospital was at Dumfries, 30 minutes' drive away. Here I was introduced to a new consultant who would look after all my dialysis needs. I was required to dialysis 3 times a week. My consultant Nadeeka came and introduced herself, and we talked about my journey so far. Nadeeka showed some concern over my blood that was still running through the neckline. The clearance was still showing elevated levels of waste in my blood and needed to be monitored closely. The next few days turned into further investigations that eventually turned into an admission to the local hospital; they said that I may have had an infection in the line, which came from the neck and travelled into the heart, which in turn carried blood back and forth once the blood was cleaned.

The main hospital in Dumfries was completed in 2017. The wards are no longer in operation nowadays. Instead, patients have a private room with en suite facilities. This was to be my home for eight weeks, including the Christmas and New Year holidays. The dialysis was still proving to be problematic, with my neck lines just refusing to flow, which in turn was reducing my clearance even more, allowing my body to be very toxic. I was assessed for infections along the heart wall on several more procedures, and all proved negative. One investigation they performed during my stay was to determine why my blood was so sticky, and even though I was prescribed blood thinners, I was still prone to blood clots. The tests confirmed that I had condition called cold agglutinin, a rare autoimmune disorder characterized by the premature destruction of red blood cells. Cold agglutinin disease (CAD) is a condition that makes your body's immune system attack your red blood cells and destroy them. It is triggered by cold temperatures, and it can cause problems that range from dizziness to heart failure. It's also called "cold antibody haemolytic anaemia." I will always remember my first days on dialysis back in 2010 when my body seemed to react in a slightly allergic way; my face would swell for no reason, causing tightening of the airways—all a very frightening episode.

As the days progressed, the only way that I could dialyze was with antihistamines, which were intravenously infused. The nurses were amazed that as the drug was administered, I would fall asleep simultaneously. A week after the Christmas holidays, I was transferred to the intensive care unit. The unit had several individual rooms covering all aspects of holistic care within the unit. There was one designated nurse who looked after all aspects of my care. I remember the room full of equipment that often sounded its alarms when needed. I was feeling a little rough, to say the least; I had headaches that were like the ones I had experienced twenty years earlier. These went on for what seemed like an age until one night everything went black. I was woken up by a nurse asking whether I was comfortable, and I tried not to move too much, as I now had Venflons in my arms and feet. I remember coming around and realizing that I was all hunched up in the bed as if in a yoga pose. Once I was comfortable in bed, the whole incident was relayed to me along with the drama that had unfolded only hours before.

I had suffered an epileptic fit. This was a first for me, and gladly the last too. There were various drugs being administered to keep my system alive during the recovery period. Over the next few weeks, access was still proving to be problematic, and new access was being talked about, which would give my system a better chance of cleaning the blood. The new access would be a Super HeRo graft, which sounds rather futuristic. This is a relatively new concept in helping patients with poor access to dialyzing. The Super HeRo graft is made of a synthetic tube that lies under the skin, connecting a blood supply from an artery, allowing a blood flow that can be used for dialysis.

Shortly after leaving Dumfries Hospital and recovering from my eight-week stay, I attended an appointment Glasgow's Queen Elizabeth University Hospital, which lies on the outskirts of Glasgow City. The hospital is a modern building built in 2010 with 1,677 beds available across all departments. I was to be admitted for three days for the new graft in my arm. Professor Kingsmore and his team were all on hand to answer any queries I may have. One of the first introductions was with the anaesthetic doctor. *Oh boy*, I thought, *here we go again, Diane's fear of being put to sleep*. I have to say the conversation and procedure I had that day regarding being put to sleep reduced and has since diminished all my fears.

After the operation, I woke in the ward with my arm all bandaged up. There was no pain or discomfort, and even the removal of the neckline was amazing; I felt free again—well, to a certain degree. Within a few hours, the bandage was removed from my arm. The nurse inspected the incision point, the inner elbow, and they had joined the graft to my artery. The graft is visible under the skin; it runs the full length of my upper arm. The nurses had been instructed to use smaller needles straight away and check the flows for dialyzing. The needle position was confirmed, and they inserted the two needles. Like the neckline used for dialysis, there is always a line that draws blood from the body, and one returns the clean blood back to the body—arterial and venous flows. Once I was attached to the machine, all the normal checks were completed, and all was running perfectly. With lunch just about to be served, I was a little wary about eating on the machine; I gingerly tried a sip of tea and jelly. It was all good, with no drop in blood pressure, and I was still in the room. I know it sounds a little strange to mention being able to eat on the machine, but not experiencing a crash or feeling a bit out of it whilst eating is huge, not only because you can enjoy lunch or tea while dialyzing but also because you are removing any food or drink from your daily allowance.

During my time at Glasgow, the nurses talked to me about self-care.

They talked to me about cleanliness and self-insertion of needles. I was super keen to learn about all aspects of the treatment process. The needles they use are all gauged on the graft that is being used for dialysis, be it an arm or leg graft, or even a fistula. The needles themselves are about an inch in length, and attached is a small plastic tube with a small connection for a syringe to be connected once the needle is inserted into the graft. The procedure of inserting the needles stings a bit, but this doesn't last long. I started to practise the correct insertion of the needles on the needle itself. I was guided on both the position and action of gliding the needles into the graft without puncturing the graft wall. As the graft was in my left arm, I was working with my right hand, which made it easier to insert the needles. I know this may be a little bit hard to believe, but inserting your needles is painless. I know, but it's so true! A handful of needles later, I seemed to have the technique mastered.

On my return to Dumfries Hospital, I was shown more about my self-care, including the machine mechanics and installing the sterile equipment used for dialysis. The inserting of my first needles was nerve-wracking but very satisfying, and I found it quite liberating to be in control of my treatment.

CHAPTER 31

The dialysis went extremely well during the following months; I felt as if I had a second wind. During the late winter of 2020, the world was hit with the COVID-19 pandemic. The first cases of COVID-19 were documented in the UK on 31 January 2020. Just as I was getting back to dialysis, the UK was sent into its first lockdown. March 24, 2020, saw new restrictions on travel and meeting friends. In the hospital, measures were taken to prevent further outbreaks, especially as a lot of the renal patients were immune compromised. During the summer months in Scotland in 2020 there were several phases that were implemented. There was no travel to visit family and friends; everything was a complete change to all our habits. A stay-at-home order was implemented, including once-a-day exercise and employees working from home when they can. Shopping turned into a completely new activity, with one-way systems in place, along with hand sanitizing on entry. The summer months were warm, so gardens, for those who had them, were luxuries. In a strange way, it made people appreciate everything they had—or had not. In Scotland, there were various phases that were implemented during the summer of 2020, with the reopening of hairdressers, pubs, restaurants, and holiday accommodation.

By December 2020, the first vaccinations were being rolled out. The second lockdown in Scotland was reintroduced on 4 January 2021, with more restrictions put into place; by April, the stay-at-home order was lifted in Scotland. By the beginning of August 2021, all restrictions in Scotland had been lifted. It was during the first summer lockdown that I really appreciated garden space; this was something I missed terribly, as the cottage I was renting didn't have a space outside. I started to look for another property locally. In November 2021, I found the perfect house with a garden, all within easy reach of the hospital for my dialysis and venturing out to see friends and family. Once settled into this two-bedroom house, I started to make it my own, arranging the furniture and filling it with ideas.

One idea I was planning was designing the second bedroom into a treatment room for my clients. In crafting this dreamy wellness haven, I went full-on perfectionist, with a luscious forest mural draping one wall and whisking clients away to Zen town. The air is perfumed with relaxing scents, and the couch is heated for extra-cosy vibes. With reflexology and ayurvedic treatments, there's something for everyone to rebalance, unwind, and cultivate harmoniously in mind, body, and soul.

Soon, the summer of 2021 ended, and we dived into the winter months. Work was steady at both home and at Brampton. As the year came to an end in 2021, I suffered a blood clot in my graft. Now, with a blood clot in a graft, it's a different scenario than when you suffer from a blood clot in your leg or lung. As grafts are additional pieces of material that carry your blood, they are not the primary supply. When a blood clot emerges within the graft, your circulatory system carries on normally. This took me into a spin. My first blood clot in my new graft was devastating, and thoughts emerged of whether this would be the end of my awesome graft, and I hoped I didn't need a neckline. To cut to the chase, a quick trip to Glasgow was arranged, and I was soon admitted to the ward. The next day, I was wheeled down to the theatre, where a nerve block was performed, and the de-clot of the graft steamed ahead. It was a very quick procedure, and before I knew it, I was back on the ward, ready for dialysis, all back to normal again and feeling fantastic.

CHAPTER 32

Spring turned to summer, and I had just celebrated my fiftieth birthday; life was amazing. I am not really a party girl nowadays; however, I still love to venture out and visit new places. Being on dialysis still has its restrictions; however, there's always a way. I hadn't planned any overseas travel, as the graft was quite new, but I felt I needed to adjust carefully if I wanted to maintain my health. Oh boy, did my parents knock it out of the park for my big milestone! They gave me a camper van, and it was like a dream come true. I could finally explore all those places I'd been dying to visit. Armed with maps and a thirst for adventure, I hit the road, scouting out the perfect spots to park up and indulge in some well-deserved me-time. Sure, I had my dialysis treatments on Mondays, Wednesdays, and Fridays, but that didn't stop me from hitting the road as soon as my Friday session wrapped up. My travels mainly took me along the Dumfriesshire coastline, where I stumbled on hidden gems galore: stunning beaches, historic castles, and crumbling ruins. And let's not forget the incredible food and drink I savoured along the way!

Three nights away in the camper van was my sanctuary; I lived in nature, making so many valuable memories. It was during one of my stays along the coastline that I was contacted by one of my clients, asking whether the gift voucher she recently purchased could be used by the recipient while I was visiting the area. Of course, I thought, *oh, how exciting reflexology is in nature.*

A date was set, and we hit the road with our shiny new tent, extending our camper van into a cosy abode. The weather was all wishy-washy, so we geared up for any surprises. And boy, were we in for a treat! The weekend was a total sizzler, and we flung open every crevice of the tent to soak in the warm sun and gentle breeze. It was pure magic! One of my clients dozed off mid-reflexology and woke up feeling like a million bucks. Thus, was born the idea of reflexology in nature, and it took off like a rocket! I continued to treat my clients outside, and soon enough we were all buzzing with a new level of energy. There's just something about nature that makes everything better!

The date was arranged, and off we travelled with a new tent that was an extension to the camper van, especially as the weather can be a bit "hitty-missy." Along with the tent and my recliner chair, I was soon on my way. As it turned out, that weekend was a scorcher, so all the parts of the tent were opened, together with warm sunshine and a light breeze. It was a beautiful experience. The client fell asleep and woke feeling refreshed and energized. Here was the birth of a new concept in reflexology in nature.

CHAPTER 33

That summer, I carried on with reflexology treatments outside, and they became extremely popular. There is a different energy for both my clients and me while practising outside in nature. The beginning of the summer of 2022 started perfectly. the camper van voyages were a total smash with the crew. Each destination, whether it was north Cumbria or a breezy beach or a serene lake, had its own unique vibe. But, during a particularly dreamy beach trip in Dumfriesshire, I sensed something odd with my arm. Normally I could feel or hear my blood pumping through my graft, but that day it was as quiet as a mouse. And before I knew it, my gut was screaming that another clot might be lurking. This suspicion was confirmed during the summer of 2022 when I discovered several graft blood clots. I found the previous clot in my arm in August 2022.

I recall feeling defeated as I realized that the graft couldn't be de-clotted any further. It felt as if we were back to square one, and my mind wandered to the episodes I'd experienced with my neckline. After exploring my options, I discovered that they were quite limited. However, after discussing with another surgeon, I learned that a leg graft might be a possibility. The only difference between the arm and leg graft was the material used. After the operation, I was heading back to Dumfriesshire, feeling like a champ. But let me tell you, the pain was no joke. With all the muscles and tendons, they had to navigate, my leg was screaming for mercy. Luckily, things started to look up once I made it to Dumfries Hospital. Their magic needles worked wonders, and I was feeling like a brand-new person! The needling was going well, and I was feeling much better.

My plans for a summer of camper van adventures were suddenly parked. It felt as though the universe had hit pause on my plans, but maybe there was a hidden silver lining. Perhaps it was time for me to recharge and rest. The universe can be a little mysterious at times, but hey, at least the weather wasn't all sunshine and rainbows that summer! I decided to take some well-earned rest after the leg graft was put in, both recuperating and relaxing at the same time. In the last few months of 2022, I returned to working my Tuesdays and Thursdays. After the New Year celebrations, I received emails from several people, some whom I knew and some who were new to me and my work. The emails I got were from clients during my time in Kelso. It's lovely to catch up with old clients; however, receiving from new clients makes my heart sing. The premise of the emails was to inquire whether I was still practising in Kelso in the Scottish borders. I currently wasn't, however, *cue a trip to Kelso*, I thought.

In April 2023, I commenced working in Kelso, and I was blessed to see both old and new clients coming through the door. Who knew that one day a week could turn into two jam-packed days a month? My reflexology skills were in hot demand, and I became a master at tapping into what the feet were whispering to me. I even kicked things up a notch with a little extra energy zing! To top it off, 2023 was a wild ride filled with border-crossing work, a wellness weekend in stunning South Cumbria with my amazing therapist pals, and let's not forget, my epic escape in the camper van! Oh, and did I mention that I was in kidney failure? No biggie, I was still playing the game of life!

CHAPTER 34

My therapy skills, if I do say so myself, have been a godsend for my soul. It's been a whirlwind of self-discovery and empowerment. My schedule was so booked that I had to up my game from one day a week to two days a month to keep up! I'm still rocking it, sticking to my niche that I found way back in 2004. I love to see what the feet are telling me; I use more energy during my reflexology nowadays. I honestly think it helps me, too, with being in kidney failure. The year 2023 was full of surprises, including my work over the border and my little energy wellness weekend which I held in south Cumbria with my amazing therapist friends. And I am not forgetting my great escape in the camper van. You must live your life to the max; I don't want regrets in my life, so I take hold of every opportunity as if it's my last. Life is a journey filled with peaks and valleys. However, by cherishing each moment and creating meaningful memories, we can gain a clear perspective of our progress and how far we have come on this incredible journey. Whilst you may decline, fear not the unexpected. Stay in your rhythm and carry on! When the challenges of life appear insurmountable, take a moment to exhale any doubts and inhale a positive attitude. It's essential to remember that nothing lasts forever, whether good or bad, and that the journey we undertake is the most significant aspect. Sometimes it's necessary to pause and unwind or pause and adjust; either way, every experience serves as a valuable lesson. We get only one body and one mind, so we must make it count!

Let's be real; food is a big part of the happiness equation. It can be the key to unlocking positive vibes, joy, and loving yourself, or it can be the mood-killer of the century. That's why it's important to fuel your body with the good stuff and keep your attitudes as delicious as your meals! To really make the magic happen, you need to have both a wholesome diet and a happy headspace. It's the perfect recipe for turning dreams into reality. Happiness is like a treasure hunt, but sometimes it feels as though the treasure is miles away from our grasp. We're so eager to seize it, but it's as if we're on a wild goose chase and every time we think we've got it, life kicks in and spoils the fun. But why can't we just keep our happy hats on all the time? Why can't we bask in the sunshine of joy every day? That's the real jackpot we're after.

Happiness is like a tricky jigsaw puzzle, isn't it? We can't just go on a wild goose chase to capture it or buy it with a bag of gold. Nope, the secret is that happiness is already inside us, waiting to be discovered. What makes you happy might not tickle someone else's fancy, and that's okay! We're all unique in our own special ways. So, let's stop chasing after happiness and take a deep breath. It's time to unleash our inner happy! Life can feel like a maze full of twists and turns that leave us bewildered, frustrated, and even frightened at times. But wait! The power to choose a different path is in our hands! By being mindful of our choices and staying aware, we can steer through any calamity, big or small. You have a superhero inside you, waiting to unleash a change that can change the world. So, it's time to grab the reins and make the magic happen!

Allow me to spill the beans about gratitude. No matter who you are, there is always something to feel grateful for, whether it's your loved ones, good health, or the book in your hand. Just the act of acknowledging these blessings flips a switch in our brains and activates the "happy chemicals"—dopamine and serotonin. This sets off a chain reaction of positivity that surges through our entire being, making us feel as if we're on cloud nine! And the best part? The more we practise gratitude, the stronger these happy neural pathways become. This makes us more self-aware and boosts our emotional intelligence. So, let's make gratitude a regular habit and feel the good vibes flowing! Writing has been a cathartic journey for me, offering moments to reflect on the power of vulnerability and authenticity. I am immensely grateful for the people and experiences that have served as my greatest teachers, even those that have tested my limits. Recognizing the value in every experience, including the challenging ones, has helped me appreciate the true meaning of happiness. Expressing gratitude has empowered me to share my stories with the hope of helping others heal, expand, and grow.

Fasten your seatbelts for 2024, because here are my powerful buzzwords! Manifesting? Yes, please! I'm diving into the deep end and making that phone call for my second transplant. I'm surrounded by a fabulous crew of wise and wonderful souls who teach me something new every day. My heart is bursting with love and affection, and I'm attracting like-minded positive peeps into my tribe. And, finally, I'm totally smitten with life! Who can predict what the future holds—am I right? But one thing's for sure: it's going to be epic! A new chapter of life is waiting for us, jam-packed with thrilling adventures just begging to be written. Let's do this!
—Your friend Diane

EPILOGUE

Buckle up for a magical ride into the future of 2024! The mystical forces of manifestation beckon, and I heed their call. With boldness and courage, I plunge into the great unknown, summoning the powers that will bring my second transplant to fruition. Guided by a tribe of brilliant souls, I bask in their wisdom and grow each day. My heart overflows with a radiant love that draws kindred spirits to my circle. And oh, how I cherish this life! Though the future remains a mystery, I am certain that it will be nothing short of epic. A new chapter awaits, brimming with untold adventures just waiting to be lived. Let's embark on this journey with joy and wonder, and see what magic unfolds!

Printed in Great Britain
by Amazon

41336215R00098